THE BOARD AND
THE PRESIDENT

THE BOARD AND THE PRESIDENT

James L. Fisher

AMERICAN COUNCIL ON EDUCATION
MACMILLAN PUBLISHING COMPANY
New York
COLLIER MACMILLAN CANADA
Toronto
MAXWELL MACMILLAN INTERNATIONAL
New York   Oxford   Singapore   Sydney

Macmillan Publishing Company
866 Third Avenue, New York, N.Y. 10022

Collier Macmillan Canada, Inc.
1200 Eglinton Avenue East, Suite 200
Don Mills, Ontario M3C 3N1

Library of Congress Catalog Card Number: 90-46409

Printed in the United States of America

printing number
1   2   3   4   5   6   7   8   9   10

Library of Congress Cataloging-in-Publication Data
Fisher, James L.
    The board and the president / James L. Fisher.
        p.   cm. — (American Council on Education/ Macmillan series on
    higher education)
    Includes bibliographical references.
    Includes index.
    ISBN 0-02-897149-3
    1. College trustees—United States.   2. College Presidents—United States.
3.   Universities and colleges.   I. Title.   II. Series:American Council on Educa-
tion/Macmillan series on higher education.
LB2342.5.F57   1991
378.1'011—dc20   90-46409
                                                                          CIP

CONTENTS

FOREWORD

Characteristic of Jim Fisher's work, this book is provocative, well-written, instructive, and entertaining. But most importantly, it represents a major challenge to mainstream thinking about university governance and predicts dramatic changes in the governance of our colleges and universities.

This book challenges most of the conventional wisdom regarding college and university governance, for it assumes that the president has been lost in the intercourse between the governing board and the various constituencies of the university, particularly the faculty.

Proceeding from this assumption, which he documents from research and by examples, he presents a careful and thorough analysis of trustee responsibilities, concentrating especially on those he considers most in need of change. These are the presidential appointment process, institutional evaluation, governance, and presidential assessment and compensation. In each of these areas, he presents models to strengthen the presidency.

While neither the Association of Governing Boards (AGB) nor I subscribe to all of Jim Fisher's conclusions, this book should be read thoughtfully by all who are concerned with the future of higher education—especially the presidency and board–president relationships.

Robert L. Gale, President
Association of Governing Boards
of Universities and Colleges

PREFACE AND ACKNOWLEDGMENTS

Increasingly, during recent years, I have felt the need to write a book about board–president relationships, something that would help to pull the center back to reason, something rooted in both systematic research and participatory decision-making that would restore the presidency to greater legitimacy.

For more than thirty years, I have watched as the relationship between the board and the president has changed, at first almost imperceptibly, and then dramatically with the coming of the egalitarian wave of the '60s and '70s.

As we attempted to wipe out the hypocrisy of race, sex, and socioeconomic discrimination in higher education, we compromised the order that made our institutions work. The roles and relationships of students, faculty, administrators, and trustees became blurred—we became a contentious group of peers, and an institution virtually incapable of substantive change. All the lines were crossed; students became masters, faculty became governors, trustees became referees, and administrators were largely lost in the shuffle, still accountable but with little real status or authority to get things done. No one was happy.

The most precarious of the lost lot were the presidents. They had been gradually stripped of any real power by governing boards who had, albeit unintentionally, acceded to faculty and student pressures for greater involvement, a euphemism for power. Presidents were left to be apologists for the unfortunate condition, or to suffer the consequences of the easily offended and often ruling family of students and faculty.

When the trouble came in the '80s and early '90s, it was the president who paid the greatest price, often his or her job. Grade inflation, no foreign language expectation, no real core requirements, no meritous consideration, a shrinking student pool, declining support, an unhappy faculty and no change; all were the fault of an unempowered leader, the president.

This book is about modifying the role of all parties, granting participation, allowing decision-making, and demanding accountability. Throughout, the fundamental governance documents in higher education are maintained (the 1940 American Association of University Professors [AAUP] Statement on Academic Tenure and Freedom and the 1966 AAUP Joint Statement on Government of Colleges and Universities). There is no recommendation in this book that cannot be documented by research and that has not been field tested. That is, I have conducted or consulted in both public and private institutions: presidential searches, institutional evaluations, presidential reviews, governance reviews, and board orientations. Additionally, I have served as a trustee for five liberal arts colleges.

I have had much help and advice in writing this book, notably: Dr. Kenneth A. Shaw, President, University of Wisconsin System; Dr. David W. Ellis, President, Lafayette College; Dr. Robert T. Conley, President, The Union Institute; Dr. James W. Koch, President, The University of Montana; Dr. George A. Pruitt, President, Thomas A. Edison State College; Dr. James L. Powell, President, Reed College; Mr. Stephen J. Trachtenberg, President, George Washington University; Dr. Roger Miller, President Millikin University; Dr. Jack Hawkins, Chancellor, Troy State University System; Dr. Douglas C. Patterson, Executive Assistant to the Chancellor, Troy State University System; Mr. Robert C. Eubanks, Jr., Chairman of the Board, University of North Carolina at Chapel Hill; Mr. George Dragas, Jr., Rector, Old Dominion University; Mr. Richard F. Barry III, Rector, Old Dominion University; Rabbi Emanuel Rose, Chairman, Board of Trustees, Lewis and Clark College; Mr. Sion A. Boney, Chairman, Board of Trustees, Hollins College. To Bob Gale and Tom Ingram of AGB, my deep admiration and affection; to my former co-workers, Martha Tack and Karen Wheeler, my appreciation for their extraordinary work on *The Effective College President*; and to Jim Murray of ACE, my gratitude for his wise advice and friendship.

My thanks to Susan Hunt for a thoughtful editing job and to my secretary, Mary Ann Rice, for coordinating the many activities associated with getting a book ready for publication. And, to my good and loving wife, Joan Fisher, for her inspiration and astute counsel.

Finally, my appreciation to the Carl B. and Florence E. King Foundation and to Mr. Carl L. Yeckel for their generous support and deep commitment to the best in education.

James L. Fisher

THE BOARD AND
THE PRESIDENT

Chapter 1

Perspective

This book, written for trustees and presidents of colleges, considers those fundamental governing board responsibilities that can ensure effective leadership. While all board responsibilities are covered, emphasis is on five key areas: the presidential appointment process, institutional evaluation, the governance design at both the board and campus levels, presidential evaluation (review), and presidential compensation. The book takes its perspective from the creditable research on effective leadership and, wherever possible, includes exhibits that illustrate appropriate practices.

Countless commissions, task forces, studies, and conferences have concluded that the current state of the college presidency is low, and precariously so. The primary reasons are the impact of a generally democratized society and the diminution of quality in all areas of higher education. The most significant result of this process, for purposes of this book, is the diminished status of the college president who, although reduced in station and authority, remains accountable to the board for the conduct of the institution.

The president is often left teetering between the faculty on the one side and the board on the other. He is accountable *for* the faculty and *to* the board, but without sufficient wherewithal to satisfy either. So, presidents come, go, or stay midst the growing lamentation of all, and boards continue to treat the symptoms rather than the problem.

Governing boards are largely responsible for the poor condition of the presidency. It is they who have approved policies and practices that have unintentionally compromised the ability of the president to lead. Boards are urged to review their policies and, if need be, restore legitimacy (authority) to the presidency.

This book is not about collegial leadership. Indeed, it documents through research that the concept of collegial leadership is, to the informed, an oxymoron. It is a proposition offered by the uninformed, by those who have never been presidents (or, if they have been, they have experienced

1

difficulty), or by those from a few institutions that have been past the need for inspiring leadership (one to two percent). For example, Harvard really doesn't need a fully legitimate president but, on its way up, Harvard was led by persons who are counted among the strongest presidents in the history of American higher education. It's a familiar pattern with many institutions: strong presidents who established them and left them prospering, only to be succeeded by "collegial" presidents who in time brought them into difficulty, until they in turn were replaced by strong presidents.

THE COLLEGE PRESIDENCY TODAY

On virtually every front, from the initial appointment process, to board policies and practices, to institutional governance, to presidential evaluation, limits are placed on the presidential office and the ability of the president to lead. The formerly legitimate conditions of presidential authority have been reduced or eliminated. Presidents are referred to as "mediators," "support mechanisms," "tinkers," "chairs," "apostles of efficiency," "faceless," "managers," "clerks of the works," and "sweepers and dusters." At the same time, conferences and commissions conclude that *the* imperative of a good future for higher education is strong presidential leadership.

Contradictions abound. On the one hand, the president is expected to lead the institution to a better condition (indeed, is usually held accountable for doing so) and, on the other, he or she receives less support, both formal and psychological, to do the job. Wherever the president turns, there seems to be a faculty or staff member, a student with a vote, or a trustee with a bent toward administration, all made legitimate by board bylaws. Accordingly, the typical board, whose policies and practices have caused this condition, is totally unaware of what it has done. I experienced this when I participated in a retreat to review the governance documents of a distinguished liberal arts college where board members were astonished at what they had approved over the years.

This lamentable situation has led national studies to conclude that "strengthening presidential leadership is the most urgent concern on the agenda of higher education in the United States" (Kerr, 1984). These groups have not gone far enough for they invariably fall short of seriously addressing a solution. In most institutions today, it would be foolhardy for a president to "lead strongly" under the precarious governance conditions that exist. One president reported, "It would be professional suicide for me to candidly address the problems of the curriculum, tenure, teaching load, or intercollegiate athletics." For some presidents, this statement has proved prophetic.

It all began with a reconstructionist movement in the early 1900s, which waned during the hard times of the Depression years and was reborn with the

wonderfully cleansing egalitarian movement of the early 1960s when reform-
ers sought to sweep out hypocrisy and install equal opportunity. This
refreshing movement left in its ebb a parity that compromised traditional form
and order and made everyone a philosopher-king. This reflects Plato's
writings about the height of the degenerate democracy, "Even the dogs
become arrogant."

As faculty members and students pressed for closer informal and formal
ties to governing boards, the nature and condition of the institution began to
change; in all things the process began to be more important than the
outcome. Faculty/student committees reported directly to boards, joint
faculty/student committees were appointed, campus governance bodies
established formal relationships with boards of trustees and assumed full
authority over academic matters. Increasingly, the president was left out of
everything but final accountability. Thus, it was only as a result of a natural
and logical progression that faculty and students began to serve on board
committees and even on governing boards and, in increasing numbers, on
presidential search and evaluation committees. The president was caught in
a squeeze.

The only thing wrong with this new process was the original assumption,
"Parity begets leadership." Like the classic paranoid personality, those who
accepted this fallacious assumption perceived everything that followed as so
logical that it defied rational objection. That this new form of participatory
governance was antithetical to virtually all of the objective research on
effective management and leadership and even contrary to classic governance
assumptions offered by the American Association of University Professors
(AAUP) was scarcely given passing consideration. "The people" had gained
the day, and most institutions soon became as politicized as the general
society.

Indeed, many board and campus governance documents stopped
mentioning the shared government statement offered by the AAUP, because
they exceeded it so far—a situation analogous to the Magna Carta or the Bill
of Rights being considered reactionary documents (see Chapter 6). Presidents
were neutered, pensioned off, or forced out of office as governing boards
blamed them for not being able to direct this fundamentally irrational process.
The leader president became the exception. Yet the basic assumption
continued unexamined.

Were the people happy? Were things better? According to surveys
reported in higher education publications and the public media, the only
group unhappier than college presidents was the faculty. According to a spate
of reports from federal and state governments, the private sector, and from
higher education itself, this rudderless unhappy state was largely responsible
for an undergraduate curriculum that had declined to an all-time low.
Conditions were so bad that by the late 1980s and into the 1990s states had
begun to mandate core academic requirements for public institutions (and the

federal government had offered *unequivocal* core recommendations). The prospect of government control had never loomed so large.

THE SOLUTION: LEGITIMIZE THE PRESIDENCY

We are aware of our problems; indeed, they can no longer be concealed. But most persist in treating symptoms. While most boards are either reluctant or uninformed about the extent of the problems, most presidents are bound to equivocate for the sake of their very jobs. National associations are, by their nature, more or less obligated to take compromise positions, and so the problem goes unaddressed as institutions continue to drift.

Instead of looking hard at the presidential appointment process, institutional governance, the true condition of the institution, presidential evaluation and compensation, and other board responsibilities, committees (often including both faculty and board members) are involved with other matters. They study the curriculum and fiscal matters, engage in strategic planning, appoint administrators, review athletic programs, and work directly with governing boards—as if any real progress could be made without a rational operating design and a university recognized legitimate leader.

In the broader sense, the restoration of presidential legitimacy is the major issue in higher education today, for without clear conditions of responsibility and authority, little can be accomplished. Research (discussed in detail in Chapter 2) clearly establishes that, except in the most exceptional cases, legitimacy is an essential condition for leadership. Legitimacy of position enhances all of the leadership forms; it makes expertise more certain, rewards more meaningful, inspiration more likely, and the use of coercion less attractive. Legitimacy grants both informality and largess for the office-holder. Expressed thoughtfully, legitimacy can make a leader out of almost anyone of reasonable sophistication and high motivation. But only the board can grant presidential legitimacy. Once it has done that, then it is up to the president.

RESEARCH ON LEADERSHIP

The review of the research presented in Chapter 2 demonstrates that the policies and practices of most governing boards are, in fact, antithetical to effective presidential leadership. The design for effective leadership described below uses a topology developed by two researchers at the University of Michigan and is increasingly accepted by others (French and Raven, 1959). John Galbraith offers a similar but less documented topology (Galbraith, 1983). Leadership is defined simply as "the ability of A to get B to do something B might otherwise not have done." All attempts to lead or influence behavior fall under one of five rubrics: (1) coercion, (2) reward, (3) legitimacy, (4) expertise, and (5) charisma.

Although measurably effective, *coercion* is the least effective form of influencing the behavior of others. It is generally used by less able persons and some long-tenured leaders whose skills are in decline.

Rewards are the second least effective form of influencing others. Although initially attractive to the new leader, specific rewards such as salary and promotion are best left to delegates, while the leader's office is reserved for review and petition. The astute leader uses more subtle rewards—letters of appreciation, kind words, and thoughtful unexpected actions.

More effective is the extent to which the leader is considered *legitimate* by those expected to be led. Yet, legitimacy can be assured *only* by the governing board. While legitimacy involves the ability both to reward and to deny, it more importantly includes the extent to which the leader is considered the *exclusive* agent of the primary authority, in this case, the governing board. If board policies include formalized contact with members of the faculty and student body, they should be changed, or the board should recognize that this condition dramatically reduces the ability of the president to lead effectively and should take this into account in its evaluation of the president.

The next two forms of leadership or power are *expert* and *charismatic* (referent), and both are considered more significant than the other three, although expertise and charisma are infinitely more effective and likely to occur from legitimate premises. Almost anyone can use coercion, reward, and legitimate power, but expert and referent power are those extraordinary, incremental qualities that mark the effective leader.

A person with expert power is, or is perceived as being, knowledgeable, and the power of knowledge is a potent factor in leadership. Although not as significant as charisma, expertise in tandem with charisma can make the leader magnificent.

Charismatic or referent leadership is the ability to inspire trust and confidence. It is significantly more influential, even in "sophisticated" communities, than all the other leadership factors combined. Nevertheless, except in the rarest of circumstances (and this book assumes none), lasting charisma can only be achieved from *legitimate* premises. That is, the leader must first be empowered and then use that position with intelligence, wisdom, and benevolence. Again, it is up to the board to grant legitimacy to the president through its policies and practices.

Charisma is best achieved by a combination of three conditions: *social distance, personal style,* and *perceived self-confidence,* the greatest of these being social distance. Social distance is the most immediately questioned leadership characteristic and the most difficult to justify without sounding pompous, secretive or manipulative. *Nonetheless, there are more research studies corroborating the importance of social distance than of any other personal leadership characteristic.* The importance and development of charisma is carefully presented in Chapter 2.

THE EFFECTIVE COLLEGE PRESIDENT

Chapter 3 presents the existing systematic research on the effective college president. Not surprisingly, the effective college president fits comfortably within the leadership profile described in Chapter 2 and derived from the generic research on leadership. Moreover, the profile of the effective college president differs markedly from that of the typical college president, having more in common with the effective corporate chief executive officer.

The effective college president is a strong, caring, action-oriented visionary who tends to act out of educated intuition. He or she is less collegial and more distant, inclined to take more risks, and likely to define effectiveness in terms of results rather than process. This profile suggests that most boards are appointing the wrong kinds of presidents.

THE PRESIDENTIAL SEARCH

It is with the presidential search that the first missteps are taken. Chapter 4 presents the problem and proposes a solution. Most presidential searches are poorly constituted and conducted. Typically, the board appoints the wrong committee, including too many faculty and not enough trustees, and ergo, the birth of the collegial presidency.

I was once asked to advise the board of a major public university. They had just weathered a difficult time during which an overly collegial president had been forced out of office by the faculty. Yet the board planned to use exactly the same imbalanced search process that had produced the previous president. A faculty committee was to screen all candidates before presenting *any* to the board search committee. After some discussion, the board changed the composition of the search committee; while it included some faculty, board members were in the majority.

A board may follow the most enlightened procedures, but if it appoints the wrong membership to the search committee, the result is bound to be either a collegial president or a compromise candidate. When faculty members are asked what kind of person they want as their president, they almost invariably respond, "Someone like us." Yet when that collegial-type president gets into trouble later, the same faculty is the first to press for presidential resignation or removal. It is an interesting cycle.

Chapter 4 discusses the presidential search process. The role of outside consultation as well as the necessity for a completely confidential search is emphasized. Using a general consultant, who becomes involved even before the appointment of the search committee, can help ensure that the cause is not lost through a poorly constituted committee or a do-it-yourself process. This chapter details the entire search from beginning to end, including institutional reviews, timetables, staff, correspondence, meeting agendas, announcements, public hearings, media relations, interview techniques, and compensation studies.

Most searches take much too long. The longer the search, the poorer the result. A college can do a good search in four months, and no search should last more than seven months, yet the typical search takes 7.2 months to complete, and some last as long as two years.

THE INSTITUTIONAL EVALUATION (REVIEW)

If the board and the president are to fulfill their important responsibility of knowing the true condition of the institution, they will need an institutional evaluation. Chapter 5 discusses this process. In an institutional review, a team of outside "authorities" (i.e.,, knowledgeable persons with no investment in the institution or its universe) evaluate the institution through reading, observing, and personal interviews, and then make appropriate recommendations. The review covers every dimension of the institution in some detail. This kind of review is *not* related to the more cursory reviews done by some search consultants as they prepare to do a presidential search, or to accreditation reports designed to ensure that the institution meets minimum standards, and not at all related to an institutional strategic plan which is bound to be too self serving.

Institutional evaluations are of special value to boards during the presidential appointment process, to new presidents as they plan their first important steps, and to sitting presidents and boards who want to assess how things are going. To my knowledge, no commissioning authority, board, or president has ever been less than enthusiastic about the value of an institutional review.

GOVERNANCE

Chapter 6, "Board and Campus Governance," emphasizes the importance of externally conducted reviews of all board policies and practices to ensure that they are compatible with the board's expectations of the president. Many boards have seen remarkable changes in presidential performance after installing new board policies. Good presidential prospects find presidencies more attractive when board policies are revised for a better order (usually as a result of an institutional or governance review).

Effective and accountable presidential leadership is clearly compatible with a commitment to the basic precepts of the 1940 AAUP *Statement of Principles on Academic Freedom and Tenure* and the 1966 *Joint Statement on*

Government of Colleges and Universities, considered the cornerstones for shared governance by virtually all in the academic community. Chapter 6 reviews both statements and demonstrates that these documents do not mandate the close associations formally adopted by so many boards; rather, these associations are the result of the gradual evolution that has led to the reduced presidency. The fault, then, is not with the documents but with the players—the faculty, the boards, and often, the president.

Appropriate conditions of governance recognize that those who are affected by decisions should have a voice in their making, subject to the final authority of the president. Under adverse conditions, the president is expected to inform the campus governance body in writing of the situation and, in cases affecting board policy, to inform the board of the position of the campus governance body. The chapter also discusses AAUP censorship and the unfortunate role of some national associations in governance.

PRESIDENTIAL EVALUATION (REVIEW)

Chapter 7 examines what is perhaps the most sensitive and delicate responsibility of a governing board, presidential evaluation or review. This is a practice now followed by some 85 percent of all colleges and universities. The typical presidential evaluation is done in a way that compromises both the presidential office and the ability of the president to lead. *The principal fault is the public involvement of faculty, students, and even staff in the process.* Over the years, such practices have led to the departure of first-rate presidents, many of whom have gone elsewhere to serve with distinction.

The evaluation is presented as a review of the condition of the institution. While the board should consider the reactions of faculty and students as it evaluates the president, the board that wishes to ensure a legitimate presidency must consider those opinions in a way that does not imply popular vote or faculty or student control.

Formal evaluation of a president should take place approximately every five years. In other years, the president and the board should develop mutually acceptable goals to serve as a basis for informal presidential review. An external consultant should conduct the formal evaluation using a design that has been reviewed to ensure that it includes suitable methods for seeking faculty and student opinion. The core of the evaluation should be interviews, supplemented by all manner of reading materials and a presidential self-review. The consultant should interview, whether in person or by phone, representatives of each of the institutional constituencies and, if possible, all members of the board.

When the consultant interviews faculty and students, the interviewees should believe they are participating in an institutional review authorized by the board and the president, rather than a presidential evaluation or assessment. Administrators and other staff should not be interviewed, for these people are, in effect, instruments of the president in accomplishing the mission of the institution.

The review should be confidential and not available to anyone except the board and the president. In states with "sunshine" laws affecting public institutions, the consultant should speak to the board in executive session (after which any notes are destroyed) or use some other equally non-public technique.

PRESIDENTIAL COMPENSATION

Chapter 8 candidly treats a subject that most presidential candidates as well as sitting presidents find awkward to discuss—compensation packages. Search committees rarely consider them, and boards often find themselves scurrying about to put together a package at the last minute before announcing the new presidential appointment. They often simply modify the current presidential compensation package. The result is a president-elect who is, at first, somewhat uncertain and later unhappy with the compensation package, but who is unable to directly address the subject.

There is no question that good candidates and incumbent presidents are often lost because of poor compensation packages. Conversely, ineffective presidents too frequently continue in office because there is no built-in graceful mechanism for leaving. Chapter 8 also discusses presidential compensation from appointment to departure. It includes sample contracts, compensation, trusts, and forms along with other appropriate strategies for improving presidential compensation in both public and private institutions.

THE RESPONSIBILITIES OF THE BOARD

Chapter 9 discusses all of the responsibilities of the governing board from the premise of the more legitimate presidency as established by research reviewed in Chapters 2 and 3. The Association of Governing Boards of Universities and Colleges (AGB) is used as the prime source, but the chapter includes additional responsibilities, combines some, and gives a different interpretation to almost all. Those responsibilities are:

1. to appoint the president;
2. to evaluate the institution;
3. to assess board policies;
4. to support the president;
5. to review the performance of the president;

6. to renew the mission;
7. to approve long-range plans;
8. to oversee the programs;
9. to ensure financial solvency;
10. to preserve organizational independence;
11. to represent both the institution and the public;
12. to serve as a court of appeal;
13. to determine board performance.

In effect, Chapter 9 accepts the classic responsibilities but advises boards to exercise them quite differently. It encourages the granting of participation in decision-making and, at the same time, allowing accountability throughout the organization. Chapter 9 discusses the dramatic differences between responsibility, authority, and accountability and challenges boards that have lost sight of the latter, accountability.

In sum, this book establishes and documents a solid research and experiential premise for effective leadership in colleges and universities and proceeds to offer a prescription for achieving that condition.

Chapter 2

Research on Leadership

Are effective college presidents different from effective corporate, political, or military leaders? Increasingly, the answer appears to be "no;" if there are any differences, they exist in shades rather than clear contrasts. In general, a leader is a leader is a leader. All leaders, then, play off the same general themes.

Leadership has been defined in many different ways, probably because through the years the subject fascinated so many scholars, all of whom approached it from countless different perspectives. Leadership characteristic studies are legion and often conflicting. Further confusing the subject are those who maintain that leadership is related to the situation rather than to the person.

Through the years, I continued to explore the subject, but remained uncertain and equivocal about it until I discovered a power topology postulated by two researchers at the Institute for Social Research at Ann Arbor, Michigan: John R. P. French and Bertram Raven (1959). I read a book by John Kenneth Galbraith, *The Anatomy of Power*, (1983), in which he had independently reached the same conclusions. At that point, my thinking, my writing, and my research on the subject became clearer. I wrote a book, *Power of the Presidency*, (1984), in which I was able to associate the various and ostensibly disparate studies on leadership under one of the five French and Raven rubrics. A few years later I co-authored another book, *The Effective College President* (1988), which was based on an Exxon-funded study of the characteristics of effective college presidents (described in the following chapter), and that study essentially corroborated my extrapolations in *Power of the Presidency*.

During this same period, I taught a seminar on leadership and power to a class of nineteen able and skeptical doctoral students. Together, we considered virtually all of the published studies on leadership and found that, without exception, each study logically fell under one or more of the French

11

and Raven power forms. We then began to formulate a definition, something both embracing and pointed.

LEADERSHIP AND POWER

Power has been defined as "the probability that one actor within a social relationship will be in a position to carry out his own will despite resistance, regardless of the basis on which this probability rests" (Weber, 1947). More simply, it may be "the possibility of imposing one's will upon the behavior of other persons" (Weber, 1947; 1954) or it may be "the ability to employ force" (Bierstadt, 1950). In the corporate world, it is defined more simply: "Power is the ability to get things done" (Kanter, 1977).

"Leadership is the basic energy to initiate and sustain action that translates intention into reality" (Bennis and Nanus, 1985). Some define leadership as the ability to influence or induce. Others define leadership as "the process of control of societal phenomena" and "the process by which an agent induces a subordinate to behave in a desired manner" and "an act in which others respond in a shared direction." John Gardner defines leadership as "the process of persuasion and example by which an individual induces a group to take action that is in accord with the leader's purposes" (1990). This definition is even more like referent or charismatic power, which we shall consider later.

French and Raven define leadership in terms of differential power, "*the ability of A to get B to do something that B might otherwise not have done.*" Twenty different but exhaustive reviews of leadership and power finally settled on this definition for both leadership and power. This is the definition I use in this book.

THE FRENCH AND RAVEN TOPOLOGY

Most researchers agree that the bases of influence are diverse, varying from one situation to another. They also agree that people use a combination of conscious and unconscious factors in attempting to lead others. For purposes of analysis, convenience, and discussion, these characteristics are elaborated on in a topology (French and Raven, 1959) since used by other researchers and adopted for this book. According to French and Raven, all forms of power or leadership fall under one or more of the following categories: coercion, reward, legitimate, expert, and referent or charisma. Some have questioned the French and Raven topology, but their objections appear unwarranted in lieu of any acceptable alternatives and because of the increasing tendency in the field to use the French and Raven classifications either directly or by other names (Bass, 1981; Burns, 1978; Galbraith,1983; and Patchen, 1974). In other words, all attempts to lead or influence use a combination of these power forms.

Before discussing these forms, we should distinguish between motives of the leader (although any motive—base or altruistic—applied intelligently, yields results). According to McClelland (1969, 1976), a person's desire for impact, strength, or influence may take either of two forms: (1) an orientation toward achieving personal gain and aggrandizement, or (2) an orientation toward achieving gain for others or the common good.

In the first instance, the need for influence is essentially self-serving and is very likely colored by unresolved achievement needs. In the second instance, the person's motivation is often labeled "socialized" (as opposed to "personalized"). He or she values the power to lead as an instrument to use for the common good on behalf of the whole organization and its members. Today, standardized tests are available to determine a person's level and type of power motivation (Hall and Hawker, 1981), but either motivation would better enable a person to lead and is essential to any dynamic movement. This book, however, focuses on leadership motivation that is "socialized", or for the common and corporate good.

One further proviso for those of an especially academic bent—this review assumes that leadership and power also embrace influence and authority, and the terms are used synonymously. It is stretching the point to assume that authority is not power, for authority without power is nothing. The effective leader will learn how to use authority and recognize its value. Indeed, leadership, influence, and authority are all a function of the intelligent use of the various power forms. To lead, to influence, and to use authority is to be powerful.

COERCIVE POWER IS MOST USED AND LEAST EFFECTIVE

Coercive power uses threats and punishments to gain compliance. Although the least effective kind of power for a leader, many would-be leaders believe that it is the key to authority. Studies indicate that the threat of punishment induces greater conformity than punishment itself (French and Raven, 1959). More recently, researchers have discovered that the leader's perceived legitimacy reduces resistance to conformity and makes punishment more acceptable to the punished. If a leader is generally admired, followers more readily accept the implied use of penalties.

But once the leader actually uses punishment, he or she becomes less effective (French, Morrison, and Levinger, 1960; Iverson, 1964). Coercion, even in its more subtle forms, invites resistance and retaliation (Kotter, 1985).

People will work harder for a leader they find attractive (charismatic) and legitimate than for one they perceive to be coercive (Zander and Curtis, 1962). Nonetheless, the threat of punishment does tend to induce compliance. It can serve as a deterrent to hostile behavior as long as the punishments are respected and/or feared (Kipnis, 1976).

We have learned that maturity tends to reduce the already questionable value of punishment as a motivating condition; that, indeed, more mature groups (e.g., university faculties) tend to be more productive under less punitive conditions (Kipnis and Wagner, 1967). However, even highly educated people are willing to administer punishment when commanded to do so by established authority figures. The Milgram studies established this to an unsettling extent (Milgram, 1965). When individuals were ordered by authority figures to administer "dangerous" degrees of electric shock to others, they almost invariably did so. There is also evidence suggesting that less confident leaders tend to rely more heavily on coercive and legitimate power than on other forms of influence (Kipnis, 1976).

It is well established that when other forms of power are wanting—that is, when an administrator is not granted sufficient authority to exercise power (by a board or an administrative superior)—he or she may be more inclined to use covert and coercive means to obtain ends (Kipnis and Vanderveer, 1971).

This condition is obvious in universities and colleges where increased authority has been given to faculty, staff, and students. Periods of tension are invariably laced with a level of suspicion and hostility that seem to justify extremes in behavior. Even during normal periods when authority is assumed by staff, the leader can no longer grant the privilege of participation, for it is simply assumed. The result: a less effective leader and a less dynamic organization.

Leaders are bound to develop diminished feelings of self-worth and reduced expectations of successful influence. This in turn leads to a greater reliance upon the use of coercion with less effective results. Under these conditions, most leaders are moved to use fear, arousal, and stealth as influence techniques (Kipnis, 1976). Clearly, as the powerholder's expectations of successful influence rise, there is an increasing tendency to exert more pressure by the use of coercive influence (Goodstadt and Hjelle, 1973).

Yet, Raven concludes that if the "goal of the leader (powerholder) is to produce long-lasting changes in behavior, then the leader would probably avoid coercive means of influence" (1974). However, if long-lasting compliance is not an issue, then the powerholder might decide to invoke stronger, more coercive sanctions. That is, in the short run, coercion may yield results, but they will not be long-lasting. If coercion must be used, it is better for the leader if punishment or sanctions are meted out by delegates who, if necessary, are later reinforced by the leader. A secure leader rarely resorts to coercive power to achieve the common good.

In summary, although the threat of punishment as penalty tends to induce compliance, an astute leader uses it seldom, if ever. On those rare occasions, research suggests that the individual punished should be isolated as much as possible from community support. Punishment should never be applied in anger or pique. Time will usually suggest another wiser and more just form of behavior that would better serve the worthy good.

REWARD POWER IS NOT AS EFFECTIVE AS MOST BELIEVE

Through reward power, a leader accomplishes desired outcomes by distributing favors, recognition, or rewards to group members. Although difficult to do, it is often better to reward those we do not like or those we feel dissimilar to than those to whom we are attracted. It is easier to influence those who are attractive or similar to us; more effort is required with dissimilar personalities.

The principal message is that the effective leader rewards those who support the goals of the organization, regardless of his or her personal feeling. Rewards are also a way to bring personality opposites into the fold. Unfortunately, leaders too often use rewards to prevent rather than to eliminate existing resistance (Lawler, 1971). Anyone who relies heavily on reward power should reward contributing supporters, but positive attention must be given to potential converts also .

The leader should not expect too much from reward power, for rewards are not likely to change attitudes permanently. Rather, as soon as rewards cease, the rewarded person probably will revert to former attitudes and behaviors (Raven and Kruglanski, 1970). Furthermore, withholding rewards results in resentment. Do not expect dramatic results from bestowing recognition, favors, or money on members of the organization. There are other leadership conditions that are far more inspiring.

Other observations support the position that reward power is a weak instrument for change (Foa and Foa, 1975). It is easy to assume that money is an effective way to ensure support, admiration, or affection, but this thinking is not attuned to human psychology. Long before there was any systematic research in the field, Machiavelli warned the Prince that "liberality" (rewards) could not guarantee that the Prince would be held in high regard by his followers. In fact, Machiavelli concluded that it was better to be feared than to try to gain support with rewards (Machiavelli, 1952).

In relatively democratic situations, coalitions almost invariably develop and parity emerges as a social principle (Thibaut and Gruder, 1969). When there is no structure (legitimate power), contractual agreements develop and power is diffused. Participants develop feelings of identification between each other, and the result is parity without discrimination and a reduction in the effectiveness of the leader (Murdoch, 1967).

In the mid–1960s, the concept of equality over equity gained even greater acceptance. More and more people found "share and share alike" to be more acceptable than the traditional notion that rewards follow personal effort and contribution. Consequently, quality and production in corporate America (profit and nonprofit) dropped to all-time lows and, according to countless reports and commissions, education—including higher educa-tion—reached its nadir. Among equals, *there are no strong leaders*.

Rewards work for the leader, but in a highly democratic society, reward-yielding situations develop feelings of responsibility for one another thus, the development of subtle informal agreements that result in greater acceptance of parity and equity rather than a sharply differentiating system of reward distribution. This kind of situation can bode difficulty for the leader who tries to reconcile the differences between merit and acquiescence.

For instance, in terms of merit pay (the only effective way to pay), the astute executive, while reserving final authority, should delegate responsibility for salaries and promotion to others, directing controversy elsewhere. There will always be controversy in such matters. (In the case of collective bargaining, reward power is so diffused that it is virtually nonexistent).

Excepting vice presidents and others in a direct reporting line, college presidents should use rewards more subtly. For example, one could use selective words or notes of praise or make appointments to key committees. There is no substitute for thoughtful, deliberate, sincere, acknowledgement and support from the leader. But positive reinforcement regarding salary and promotion is the wisest choice. Use merit pay, but let others do it. Most importantly, bear in mind always that there are limits to the secure and effective use of rewards. Worthwhile support cannot be bought.

LEGITIMATE POWER IS THE LEADER'S PLATFORM

To be most effective, the leader needs structure, form, station, authority, protocol (a position from which to be inspiring), compassionate, giving, and charming. Legitimate power is the leader's platform. The effective leader should get on that platform and stay there. Once there, the leader can negotiate the platform with warmth, sincerity, and benevolence. The leader must accept the prerequisites of authority and position and, from the first day, appear to live comfortably with them. The leader should never apologize for or downplay a position. To do so is simply a way of telling others that you do not deserve the office, and it certifies a less effective performance.

Legitimacy is based on a group's acceptance of common beliefs and practices. The acceptance of these practices and beliefs, which include the distribution of influence within the particular setting, binds those members together through their common perspective. The group adheres to leaders who appear to fit certain roles which are consistent with their expectations, endowing those persons who assume leadership with certain power. For instance; general, chairman, mother, judge, president, manager, doctor, dean, priest, senator: all of these titles within a given context grant legitimate power to the individual.

Certain activities and actions come to be expected and accepted from those leaders and are considered legitimate. "In all cases, the notion of legitimacy involves some sort of code or standard accepted by the individual by virtue of which the external agent can exercise his or her power" (French and Raven, 1959).

Some consider this condition authority rather than power (Burns, 1978; Pfeffer, 1981), while others style it leadership. For our purposes, the acceptance of common norms enables a leader to exercise power that otherwise might not be accepted by the group. *By so legitimizing power, its exercise is transformed in a remarkable way, for it makes the use of all other leadership forms (coercive, reward, expert, and charismatic) more acceptable to the group.*

For instance, in most social situations, the exercise of power involves costs. We pay the cost of resources, make commitments, and have a greater need to rely on the other power forms. In effect, the leader uses up potential for influencing the group, because in most situations, parity of opinion prevails. Without legitimate authority, all players are expected to take turns on center stage.

Clearly, the possession of legitimacy or authority will be, if used effectively, a significant enhancement in the effectiveness of the leader, for it will not cost him or her other power forms. Indeed, people in legitimate authority positions are expected to use their authority, and at times are even punished for not doing so (Dornbusch and Scott, 1975). But most newly appointed executives are afraid to exercise the limited authority they have. Their anxiety and uncertainty make them say, "Wait awhile until I get the lay of the land." By the time they realize their mistake, it's too late. This initial uncertainty has long-lasting effects on the executive's ability to become a leader.

Conversely, often too little legitimacy is given to those who are expected to lead. Bosses and boards limit the authority of a legitimized figure, and then wonder why the person can't produce up to expectation (Burns, 1984; Kanter, 1977; Kotter, 1985). During recent years, this has happened to countless executives in industry, education, and government. Stripped of legitimate authority, they find it almost impossible to lead.

People generally follow legitimate leaders with whom they agree. Those with whom they disagree are likely to be ignored, subverted, and finally, sent packing. That is the reason expert and charismatic power are so important to the leader (which will be discussed later). While legitimacy is a significant element of influence and control, like coercive and reward power, it is not as effective as most people think. The leader needs more than legitimacy. People who do not at least reluctantly agree with their leader often disobey or ignore him or her. In extreme cases, they even try to overthrow the leader. Legitimate leaders who noticeably overstep the bounds of their roles invite resistance.

A common and troublesome situation arises when a delegate leader does not discharge his or her office. I term this a "power vacuum," the antithesis of a competent application of leadership principles. It is all too often characteristic of university administrators. It occurs when the appointed leader, for whatever reasons—usually collegiality—does not assume the responsibilities of the office. This condition, coupled with other compromised standards, makes for apathy, frustration, and finally resentment. Assignment to a legitimate leadership role does not confer any leadership abilities, only the potential for leadership. Unfortunately, an individual who is placed in a decision-making position may become paralyzed. Others then assume, diffuse, and diminish authority until there is none. During this period, both production and morale always drop.

Nonetheless, it is important to emphasize that within formal organizations such as universities and corporations, norms and expectations invariably develop that make the exercise of power expected and accepted. Thus, reasonable (and sometimes even unreasonable) control of behavior becomes an expected part of corporate life. Legitimate power is of fundamental importance to all who would be leaders. *This is because once power becomes legitimized it will not be resisted unless it is abused or ineffectively used.*

Once power becomes legitimate, it no longer depends on the resources or arguments or power that produced it in the first place. It can stand alone. Indeed, the more legitimate the leader becomes, the more the group accepts the leader, and the greater it judges his or her competence. The more legitimate the leader, the more the leader is endowed with superior personal qualities (Clark, 1956; Hollander, 1961; Pepitone, 1958; Sherif, 1953; Sherif, White, and Harvey, 1955). Thus, the more legitimate the leader, the more effectively he or she can exercise the wonderful "incremental" forms of leadership that follow: expertise and charisma.

Holding a position of high status does not automatically make a leader; it simply provides a great advantage to the effort. The higher the leader advances, the more care he or she should take in resisting the tendency toward detail, inflexible procedure, and a custodial mentality (Gardner, 1990). These are the kinds of things behind which the unsuccessful hide.

Legitimacy is maintained, then, not so much by its originating sanctions but rather by the degree to which the group continues to adhere to the common and unifying bonds that produced the legitimate leader in the first place. If a holder of legitimate power—such as a corporate officer, a judge, a store manager, or a college president—conducts the office poorly, then power again becomes diffused. The group spends more time in conflict than in growth. Legitimate power adds stability to the group and can be used most effectively after the leader thoroughly understands and appreciates the other forms of power (leadership).

Research has also established that group members perceive an organization's status structure and production potential effectively when high-status members react less extensively throughout the organization but retain final authority. That is, the effective leader is not the "good buddy" type. Rather, the leader moves around the organization frequently, being warm and friendly, but not overly involved or intimate, and always remaining on the platform. The president is always the president.

Indeed, legitimate power largely depends on the extent to which group members perceive the leader's role in the first place, and they cannot perceive someone who is overly involved with them as an inspiring leader (Scott, 1956). People are less inclined to be resentful and hostile when they are operating under common and understood norms with fully legitimized leaders.

Although there is conflicting research, appointed leaders are generally considered more legitimate and effective than elected leaders (Bass, 1981; Julian, Hollander, and Regula, 1969). Rather than making a leader more secure and effective, election generally tends to result in anxiety, insecurity, and vulnerability.

One further word: the recent documentation of the loss of public confidence in most contemporary institutions has consequences for decision-making in all corporate life. The acceptance of some form of authority is critical to all forms of organizations, from the family group to the most "collegial" university. If there is no authority, during times of difficulty the organization proves ineffective and either disintegrates or is replaced. Indeed, Burns makes a compelling case for increasing the legitimate authority of the U.S. presidency because of the government's inefficient, and now obsolescent, system of checks and balances (Burns, 1984).

As we have established, it is impossible to exercise control of general direction by using only rewards and punishments (although both are legitimizing power agents). Also, it can not be done with consistent effectiveness by using only expert or even charismatic influence. It is essential to have a legitimate power base with sufficient authority to back it up.

Even anthropologists advise us that while thrones may be out of fashion, authority still requires a cultural frame in which to define itself and advance its claims (Geertz, 1983).

Legitimacy allows the leader to make choices in a fashion that approximates the rational model (Pfeffer, 1981). When authority erodes through the loss of confidence and legitimacy, followers are less likely to accept decisions without question. What was once a rational process for decision-making becomes a political struggle that can be the very undoing of the organization itself.

It takes a masterful, legitimate leader to overcome the currents of the general society. This is the case with corporate leaders under conditions of extreme unionism, religious leaders during periods of demysticism, and political and educational leaders during periods of egalitarianism. Because everyone has a piece of the action (power), little or nothing gets done. The tyranny of the many is every bit as debilitating as the tyranny of the few.

In sum, legitimate power is essential for the effective leader. People tend to accept a legitimate leader when they agree with his or her policies and actions. The legitimate leader will be effective to the extent that he or she appreciates and uses the various other forms of leadership. Most reasonably intelligent and educated people can be effective legitimate leaders. Although election to a leadership role is preferable to becoming a leader, being appointed seems to be the best way of all to ensure effectiveness. Leaders who present themselves as being legitimate tend, in fact, to be more effective. They are generally better liked and their attempts to influence are better accepted.

The discussion of expert and charismatic power that follows represents a kind of "incremental power" characteristic of an individual. Legitimate, reward, and coercive power tend to be organizationally derived. That is, the legitimizing agent (governing board, corporation, country, religious organization, society itself) enables the leader to hold position and to reward or punish, but it is the extraordinary person who weaves in these next two near magical forms of power. Most people of reasonable ability and motivation can exercise the first three forms of power. But those who adroitly use charismatic and expert power will be the most effective leaders.

EXPERT POWER IS KNOWLEDGE OR ITS FACSIMILE

Expert power, which reflects the deference accorded a perceived authority, tends to further legitimize leaders and make them more effective (Goodstadt and Kipnis, 1970). Expert power in most circumstances is the most consistently effective power of those discussed so far. There are two ways to wield the influence of an expert: to be introduced to a group as an expert (unless you make a monumental mistake, you will be the controlling influence in the group); or to actually become an expert, a person who is knowledgeable and informed about the subject at hand. The difference between the two may be obscure to observers, who are inclined to accept expert power uncritically. For instance, Lowe and Shaw found that, even though authoritative attempts to predict the future were sometimes inaccurate, the forecasts were accepted and influential in decision-making because of the confidence and perceived expertise of the forecaster (1968, in Pfeffer, 1981). It is also true that appearing to withhold information or expertise is a measurably significant power form (Pettigrew, 1972, in Pfeffer, 1981).

Clearly, as a leader attempts to garner support for a particular cause, it is valuable to be perceived as an expert. This perception both inspires support for a common cause and reduces unproductive conflict. People frequently accept expert pronouncements because it takes time and effort for an opponent to gather information for an alternative position. Most are not willing to risk the loss of popularity involved in going against the confident leader.

Research further demonstrates the value of perceived expertise. People introduced as prestigious feel better accepted and more at ease than people assigned low-prestige roles. They are measurably more effective and influential. (People introducing speakers should get this message.)

Groups with more than one expert are less certain of their judgment, and even the experts are less effective (Collanos and Anderson, 1969). This echoes the Marine Corps adage, "It's better to have one idiot in charge than two geniuses." The more acknowledged experts in a group, the less effective their expert powers. Even the experts become inhibited. In groups with many experts, high status (legitimate power) rather than expertise can be a more significant determinant of behavior (Torrance, 1955). Combining expertise with high position is a most effective posture, providing the leader demonstrates expertise consistently. Therefore, key executives should rarely speak in groups unless they are certain of their subject material. The effective leader no longer enjoys the luxury of spontaneous brilliance or foolishness.

In sum, knowing more about a subject than others, combined with the legitimacy of position, gives an incumbent a decided advantage in any situation. The leader should always try to be perceived as knowledgable, which means that he or she rarely participates in groups of other experts, delegates as many details as possible, always strives for greater expertise, and often refrains from speaking. The main job of the leader is to inspire, occasionally offering a trace of detail merely to imply greater knowledge. But if wrong or mistaken, he or she should admit the error at once, without dwelling on it. The leader who bullishly refuses to acknowledge mistakes or overlooks them suffers a loss of all of the most effective leadership forms.

CHARISMATIC (REFERENT) LEADERSHIP IS THE MOST EFFECTIVE FORM OF POWER

Charismatic leadership, the single most effective form of leadership, is based on the admiration and liking that people feel toward an individual. The charismatic leader has an extraordinary ability to inspire trust and confidence. Some researchers have used the term "referent power" for this category, and others have used the terms "heroic" or "charismatic." I prefer charismatic, in spite of its sometimes uncomfortable connotations. This is not the charisma of divine inspiration, a special gift, grace, or talent that some have and most have not, but rather a quality of trust and confidence that almost anyone can honestly cultivate.

For centuries, philosophers have viewed gaining the affection, trust, and respect of others as the most effective form of leadership. Throughout history and literature, we can find people who have become heroes by winning the adulation of others. People feel secure with these heroes; some go so far as to become worshipful (Geertz, 1983). People like Eisenhower and MacArthur became heroes and then charismatic leaders. Today, researchers are increasingly able to document that those characteristics referred to as "charismatic" constitute the behavior that is most effective in inspiring others to follow and support a leader (Foa and Foa, 1975; Galbraith, 1983; Geertz, 1983; House, 1977; Machiavelli, 1952; Mott, 1970). Clearly, someone who is respected and trusted by others is most able to exert influence over them. (Tedeschi, Lindskold, Horai, and Gahagan, 1969).

The way to lead people beyond the limited capacity of more conventional leadership forms, and even beyond themselves, is to study charismatic leadership and then learn to use it ethically. One needn't feel uncomfortable at the thought of wanting to be respected and admired, for increasingly, researchers are concluding that this urge relates more to the need to accomplish high goals than to ego gratification (McClelland, 1976).

People want to agree with and to follow charismatic leaders (they often twist their own logic to agree with a leaders position). Followers defend a charismatic leader when he or she is not present and take strong exception to those who unfairly criticize the leader. (Some "friends" won't do that.) People who follow charismatic leaders are convinced that things will get better, whatever the condition, and they always feel better about themselves (French and Snyder, 1959).

The most effective leader is one who combines charismatic power with expert power from a legitimate power base, adding carefully measured portions of reward power and little or no coercive power. For their part, the followers subordinate their own interests to those expressed by the charismatic leader. This creates a symbiotic relationship in which followers translate the visions of the leader into existence. The personal influence coming from charismatic power both complements and exceeds the impression made by position, rewards, penalties, and expertise.

Indeed, charisma can often produce results without calling from other more common methods of power. Most people want to cooperate and to be part of an exciting and potentially significant activity. They seek a mission in life beyond their personal dreams. The leader who takes advantage of all the dimensions of rational charisma provides this mission. The duration of effective leadership depends almost exclusively upon the leader's ability to use charismatic power (Falbo, 1977)

Invariably, effective leadership seems to be rooted in charismatic qualities rather than in other leadership forms or in more traditional factors.

This impression is as valid among highly educated groups, which assume a peer relationship, as among the less educated. Although groups of people with complex personalities change leaders more often, sophisticated people are just as prone to succumb to the appeal of power figures as others (Schroder, Streufert, and Weeden, 1964). In fact, they will often go to ridiculous lengths to gain their acceptance (Hurwitz, Zander, and Hymovitch, 1953; Jones and Jones, 1964). Even other high-status figures cooperate with and become followers of the charismatic leader (Slusher, Rose, and Roering, 1978).

The leader can dramatically increase his or her influence by recognizing and responding to the fact that people are attracted to those with power. Followers are especially loyal if association with a perceived authority figure seems to offer a chance to enhance their own reputation or status. It is a wise leader who provides opportunities for reputation-building and the empowerment of others (Kanter, 1983).

The leader is more easily perceived as charismatic when viewed from a more distant vantage point (Hollander, 1978). Thus, the value of the podium, the stage, and the movie screen. Charismatic influence is more effective in structured than in unstructured situations (Cohen, 1953, 1959). In unstructured settings, attractive personal qualities are less likely to influence behavior (Godfrey, Fiedler, and Hall 1959). Structure firmly sets limits and priorities and establishes positions, thus, further reinforcing the importance of legitimate power to the leader. These are optimum conditions for the leader, within which he or she can exercise familiar behavior with those to be led without compromising the position of authority. Structures, however, should come before familiarity, and even then there should be only limited familiarity. Power is structurally determined, but it is also affected by the leader's capacity to convince followers of his or her value and importance. The charismatic leader who inspires trust and confidence makes other people feel valuable as well (Pfeffer, 1981).

An imprecise mission tends to yield to a leader a comparatively high degree of influence and control over group behavior (Smith, 1973). Under these conditions, even if the leader fails to achieve specific goals, people become more accepting, display higher satisfaction, and maintain support for the leader. Vague but lofty goals are good insurance for the leader. Outstanding leaders are considered persons of great vision. People are more likely to feel comfortable, rewarded, and to be supportive if they perceive the leader as both important and yet somewhat mysterious. While there should be measurable goals and specific objectives, they should be subordinate to the quest to be the most effective and to have an achievable and empowering vision (Kotter, 1982, 1988). The effective leader approaches the job with overall ideas and high goals, rather than concrete plans.

These are the five power forms of the effective leader: coercive, reward, legitimate, expert, and referent or charismatic. Effective leadership is totally dependent on the extent to which the leader understands, develops, and astutely uses a sensitive combination of these power forms. The greatest of these is charisma, the ability to inspire trust and confidence. A charismatic presence can best be developed from a strong base of legitimate and expert power. The leader always makes the most of position and never stops learning the trade.

THE DEVELOPMENT OF CHARISMA

Despite popular opinion, there is nothing genetic or intuitive about charisma—the ability to inspire trust and confidence. Anyone of reasonable intelligence and high motivation can develop charismatic characteristics. Age, gender, race, height, weight, and other obvious personal characteristics have little or nothing to do with the ability to develop and use charismatic influence. Virtually anyone of reasonable intelligence and strong motivation can accomplish it.

Many factors contribute to charisma: sincerity, appearance, focus, confidence, wisdom, courage, sensitivity, discipline, vision, reliability, and strength. After reviewing almost every published study on the subject, I have concluded that these traits fall under three principal categories: distance, personal style, and perceived self-confidence. The most clearly document-able of the categories is distance, specifically social distance.

THE IMPORTANCE OF SOCIAL DISTANCE

Although it may seem an uncomfortable concept at first, the most certain requirement for charisma, distance,* becomes more acceptable as it is understood. Day-to-day intimacy destroys illusions. Daily contact consequently makes charisma more difficult to establish at the lower level of most organizations. The man or woman immediately above, with whom you work and talk every day, may have many strengths. But frequent contact obscures the strengths, emphasizes the weaknesses, and obliterates charismatic impressions. That is why a leader's closest associates, in the long run, offer the greatest test of leadership.

The leader should try to appear on important occasions and to be present often, but briefly, in the workplace. The leader shows up for

---

*Distance, taken to the extreme as a personal lifestyle, can lead to serious problems. But, to my knowledge, there is no research that concludes that too much distance is a problem for people who want to be leaders. While many effective leaders are considered overly remote, and distant, this condition almost invariably helps the leader, who can then demonstrate unusual humanness by occasional forays into the open. Too many exposures, however, make the leader overly familiar to those he or she would lead.

celebrations and, in times of sadness, knows where the coffee-pots are, but doesn't stay too long anyplace. The leader always remains sufficiently remote and doesn't let modesty, fear of embarrassment, or naiveté get in the way of accomplishing the mission.

Some would-be leaders, particularly those in large and complex organizations, may allow the bureaucracy (or whatever the "system" is called) to overwhelm them. If they are unwilling to rise above those structures, they become little more than coordinators who dare to work only at the fringes of their organizations. (Indeed, there are some in higher education who believe that this is all a college president can really do.) They may survive, but they rarely win. They often feel that real leadership is impossible in such settings. Exactly the opposite is true. Effective leadership is both easier and of longer duration in large organizations than small ones.

Arthur Schlesinger and Richard Neustadt discussed this problem in their analysis of the U.S. presidency (Neustadt, 1960). They used Franklin Roosevelt as an example of a president who would not allow himself to become captive to the complexity of the office. Roosevelt was close enough to the group to permit personal identification but sufficiently removed to be perceived as mystical. He was perceived as a superior and inspiring figure. It is precisely this mystical quality that encourages those being led to attach themselves to the leader's personality and to reach beyond their everyday expectations.

Some may find the concept of distance distasteful. Anyone deliberately using such a stance for personal advantage might seem calculating, even dishonest. How can it be right to be less than open, less than completely honest? Aren't trust and confidence rooted in complete revelation and the exchange of intimate feelings? The answer to these questions is *no*, not if you want to lead and inspire others. Think of the good relationship between parent and child, teacher and student, religious leader and congregation, or even between intimate friends. Think of the priest who is warm and friendly, but always remains the priest. Think of those countless relationships that bind human beings together and that involve and even depend on "distance."

Leaders who admit full personal parity with those they are to lead invite uncertainty, anxiety, confusion, and often chaos. Families, nations, congregations, companies, and classrooms have been devastated for want of respect. Respect must be earned, but it is also a product of values and tradition, and it is best sustained through distance. A parent or teacher or any leader must maintain enough closeness to promote understanding, but enough distance to be respected.

Familiarity often breeds unproductive controversy. Distance is essential, for it allows those at the various levels in an organization to maintain reasonable order and ensure progress. The effective charismatic leader maintains optimal psychological distance from subordinates. The leader is neither close enough to be hampered by undue emotional ties nor so distant that emotional contact is lost.

The leader must find the proper balance. Remember, however, that most are more likely to err on the side of being overly familiar rather than too distant. The leader should initiate the drive for familiarity, always keeping in mind that familiarity breeds debate, questions, doubts, and reservations. Leaders are essentially no different from followers, and they should never think otherwise. A good example of this point is a religious leader. One minor lapse in conduct can jeopardize such a person's image as a moral, thoughtful, and controlled leader. Successful leaders will not allow an office to be devalued, either by themselves or by others. If anyone else exceeds the bounds of propriety in the presence of such a person, the demeanor of the effective leader abruptly negates this depreciation.

High-status people in close association with others in their organization tend to compromise the stated goals of their organization more readily than others: the higher the office, the more likely the leader is to compromise (Mills, 1953). Authority figures who yield too readily to their group are more likely to be exploited by the group (Swingle, 1970). This suggests that the leader should maintain psychological distance from the members of the group. Nice guys, at least to the degree that they compromise their office, do finish last. The idea of consensus or collegial leadership in this light is ludicrous, particularly during times of conflict and tension.

Distance has been a characteristic of effective leaders throughout history. There needn't be anything dishonest or unethical in distancing. Unless the leader is absolutely, unimpeachably wonderful (and who is?) it is unwise for him or her to establish intimate relationships with members of the affected organization. Of course, some leaders will always be tempted to test this precept, and they will be exceedingly fortunate if those relationships don't come back in haunting ways.

Distance means being utterly open but always remote. Distance is having a close associate, who has known you for ten years and would say, "Yes, he's my best friend and I would do virtually anything for him, but I can't say that I completely know him."

Distance is recognizing that a leader is no longer "one of the boys or girls." It is being a friendly presence: warm and genuine, concerned and interested, but rarely around too long and rarely getting too involved. Distance recognizes and uses the trappings of office, adjusting them only to suit the personality and sophistication of the audience or constituency. Distance balances remoteness with familiarity. The effective leader appears both excitingly mysterious and utterly known. Distance involves being warm and attentive, open and casual, but never, never getting off the leadership platform with anyone the leader expects to influence.

As long as the leader realizes that he or she is not really any different, except in perspective, from anyone else, distance will not become arrogance. From time to time, aware leaders laugh at the reassuring thought that they are personally so insignificant. There is also a practical reason for this: the leader who takes the image too seriously or becomes self-serving will soon be found out and become less effective. In time, this leader will lose the most vital element in charismatic influence: the trust and confidence of followers. A lack of sincerity or commitment invariably shows itself to others.

The message here is that if the leader loses interest, he or she should leave. The greater the effort to conceal the truth, the more transparent the lie. The greater the need to fabricate, the less attention given to nonverbal clues that are the first sign of the faltering leader.

The connecting force between the leader and the followers is an emotionally charged relationship. Leaders are idealized as those whose strength enables them to assume the responsibility for their followers. Who else can better devise solutions and direction? Even the most sophisticated of followers may deny that leaders experience doubts, insecurities, or weaknesses. Followers react to their leaders' human foibles with disbelief, astonishment, dismay, and even anger. It's as if they were saying, "If you are not totally dependable, then you may not be dependable at all." Effective leaders may safely drop their reserve only with intimates who accept their humanness and who have no motive for placing them in idealized positions or roles of omnipotence.

Vision is also a key characteristic of the effective leader and a valuable dimension of social distance. Vision is having and holding a goal, a commitment, even a dream that is greater than the organization itself, and possessing certain ideas about how the dream can be achieved. Father Theodore Hesburgh, President Emeritus of the University of Notre Dame, was recently named the most effective college president in America. When a *USA Today* reporter asked him, "Why?" Father Hesburgh (after first asking for a recount) paused and answered simply, "The vision." Indeed, there is no single characteristic so common in outstanding leaders.

The effective leader sustains the vision and does not allow it to be swallowed up by time and specific plans. When associates begin to lose sight of the vision and get caught in the corporate maze it is the leader who must raise their sights. The dream must always be there first; specifics will evolve, but they only serve to accomplish the dream.

RESEARCH SUPPORTS SOCIAL DISTANCE

Let's look more closely at the research. Numerous studies and reports demonstrate the value of both social and psychological distance in effective leadership (Fiedler, 1967; Fiedler, Obrien, and Ilgen, 1969; Hill, 1969; Hunt, 1967; Julian, 1964, Pfeffer, 1981; and Burns, 1978). All support the hypothesis that social distance relates positively to productivity.

Blau and Scott (1962) and others have concluded a report that distance between leader and followers strengthens group ties. Stogdill reports Burke's 1965 research, which found that high-need achievement followers with low social-distance leaders rate their situations as more tense, regardless of the nature of the task. Stogdill then presents twenty-one studies demonstrating that psychological distance between leader and followers increases group productivity (Rubin and Goldman, 1968). Later, Bass further confirmed Stogdill's conclusions (Bass, 1981). In other words, productivity tends to be higher under leaders who maintain social and psychological distance between themselves and their followers.

As early as 1955, Shepherd and Weschler found that distance between the leader and followers resulted in fewer communication difficulties. When leaders worked side by side with subordinates, particularly in formal organizations, there were greater communication problems. Even authoritarian leaders who are relatively distant are more influential than others. Thiagarajan and Deep studied three types of leaders—authoritarian, persuasive, and participative. They found that authoritarians were most powerful and the participative least powerful (Thiagarajan and Deep, 1970). It appears that groups tend to follow leaders who have a combination of a sense of office and a persuasive style. It should come as no surprise that followers gain security when they are associated with a strong leader. Individuals are conditioned to respond to clearly defined roles.

Despite this evidence, there are still skeptics. A distinguished college president reviewed an earlier book of mine that addresses this subject (Fisher, 1984). She described the book as "fascinating, and instructive but somewhat perverse," but she did not seem to acknowledge the research premise for the assumption. I understand her misconception. I know that distance may be an uncomfortable premise, but it should not be abandoned easily. Others mistakenly generalize about charisma in its most extreme forms (Reverend Jim Jones, the Ayatollah Khomeini, etc.). Thus, they bring the entire concept into question and dramatically reduce the acceptability of this power form.

People perform more effectively when they like and esteem their leaders. Esteem for the leader is more likely to produce high performance among followers than the followers' esteem for each other. Followers like to be liked by high-status figures and will use subtle ingratiation techniques (Jones, Gergen, Gumpert, and Thibaut, 1965).

The higher the perceived status (legitimate power) of the leader, the more likely the group is to revere and accept him or her. Thus, status differences lead to psychological and social distance (Bass, 1981). A little self-disclosure by a leader will likely do more harm than good. For example, when people of presumed high status offer personal anecdotes, they compromise their status and reduce their leadership effectiveness. We expect our leaders to be superhuman, to be far superior to the rest of us. All would-be leaders should remember this; just don't take it personally.

Seeman found that when public school teachers rate their principals high in status and perceive wide differences between their own status and that of the principal, they tend to like the principals and to rate them high in leader effectiveness (1960). Scott's research suggests that effective leadership and achieving distance are best accomplished when leaders operate less extensively throughout the organization yet retain final authority (1956). That is, the leader is everywhere and nowhere.

PERSONAL STYLE AND CHARISMA

Style is a related characteristic that distinguishes a leader from the pack, but not so much as to be unique. There is not as much evidence of its effectiveness as there is for distance, and therefore it is a more debatable characteristic. Style combines many things: energy, visibility, decision-making, humor, trust, integrity, dress, appearance, and personal habits. Style is that fortifying inner sense that allows the leader to be individualistic. Above all else, it does not pander to every popular appetite and fancy, or attempt to be all things to all people.

It is true with great legitimate power a person can convincingly affect almost any style, regardless of how singular. For instance, very wealthy or high-status people can often get away with peculiarities in behavior or dress. This may also hold for distinguished professional/author/artist types. But it rarely applies to college presidents or corporate and political leaders, except possibly those of long tenure and exceptional accomplishment. Most shouldn't chance it.

Leaders comport themselves as if they have high energy. Boundless energy, limitless enthusiasm, and persistent dedication enable others to embrace the dream. Unfortunately, most effective leaders marry their vision and thus spend inordinate amounts of time either working or thinking about their responsibilities. Herman Wells, President Emeritus of Indiana University, wrote "My whole being was concentrated on this work; yet. . .it was so challenging that extraordinary effort was not only possible but exhilarating. The refreshment received in turning from project to project dispelled the tedium" (Wells, 1980). Wells was a bachelor, other presidents have jeopardized their health and their marriages with such a commitment.

The effective leader usually adopts a visible style. Peters and Waterman refer to visibility as "management by walking around" (1982). Mortimer and McConnell write that in colleges and universities, "Unseen administrators will only become targets of anger and hostility in crises, because unfamiliarity (of this kind) breeds contempt" (1978). Cox goes even further, saying that would-be leaders who stay in their offices are "making a workstyle decision that is personally stultifying and harmful to the enterprise " (1985).

Conversely, numerous writers, including psychologists, have cautioned the leader to keep in check the desire for personal recognition (Astin and

Scherrei, 1980; Birnbaum, 1988; Drossel, 1981; McClelland and Burnham, 1982). Birnbaum advises the "cybernetic" leader to be modest (1988 p. 200). It is important that the visibility of the leader serve the best interests of the mission and not the individual. The leader will know when the line is crossed. The visible leader not only shares the credit, granting the greater portion to others, but shares visibility as well.

Effective leaders recognize that visibility enhances their effectiveness and engenders confidence in both their institutions and themselves as leaders. They seem to sense when to be seen and when to maintain a low profile. They also know that in acknowledging others, they enhance their own images, develop constituent loyalty, and, most importantly, more nearly accomplish the mission.

As the research on social distance indicates, the leader has warm, but not intimate, relationships with a large number of people. He or she is concerned about the worth and dignity of each individual. In higher education the effective president is "people oriented, caring, supportive, and nurturing" (Gilley, 1986). Cox writes that "warmth is not only the province of the do-gooders and the naive, but also of top executives who are [successful]" (Cox, 1985). The successful leader "sees the best in his people not the worst; he's not a scapegoat hunter" (Walker, 1979).

The effective leader has superb communication skills. In his pioneering piece on the college presidency, Thwing writes extensively about good interpersonal and communication skills. "The president should be free from cantankerousness, have tact, and should emphasize the merit of associates" (Thwing, 1926). A number of writers in higher education emphasize accessibility and listening as key elements in leadership style (Birnbaum, 1988; Dressel, 1981; Green, 1988; Townsend, 1985; Vaughn, 1989).

The charismatic leader acts out of a kind of informed insight. While the leader is not quick to make decisions, he or she is a bold decision-maker. Although recognizing the long-range planning, the charismatic leader does not allow the vision to get bogged in planning for the future. This leader is more interested in inspiring consensus than in measuring—a very different approach from that of the uncertain leader. (Bennis, 1989; Bennis and Nanus, 1985; Kotter, 1977; Peters and Austin, 1985; Peters and Waterman, 1982; Townsend, 1985). Bennis and Nanus say it well: "Effective leadership takes risks—it innovates, challenging and changing the basic metabolism of the organizational culture" (1985). Peters and Austin note that it is "hanging on after others have gotten bored or given up" (1985). Whetten calls risk-taking "aggressive opportunism" (1984). At some point the leader must say, "Ready, fire, aim."

Bass speaks of the transformational leader who "is less willing to be satisfied with partial solutions or to accept the status quo" (1985). The inspirational leader will press for what is right or good, not necessarily what is popular or acceptable according to the established wisdom of the time.

The charismatic leader is both trusting and trustworthy. Gardner emphatically calls for leaders to build trust within their organizations (1990). Fairness is perhaps the most important condition of trust and must be considered with every decision. Leaders use a kind of "ethical" integrity and honesty to build trust throughout the organization (Wenrich, 1980). They couple all of this with a healthy and spontaneous sense of humor. They do not take themselves too seriously, at least not for long. When they do, they are able to laugh at themselves.

Effective leaders in business, industry, or higher education believe in and use shared decision-making. They believe that things are better when those affected by decisions have a voice in their making. While retaining final authority, they use this authority gently.

Leaders rarely give orders or tell people what to do (Kotter, 1988). They truly listen to the people in their organization and often count their opinions more important than their own (Peters and Austin, 1985). They are politically astute, pragmatic and skillful bargainers (Whetten and Cameron, 1985). Shared decision-making is not necessarily collegial or consensus decision-making, for in any effective organization lines of responsibility, authority, and accountability must be maintained.

Dress and appearance enhance style. In most corporate settings, including higher education institutions it is important to dress conservatively; men should wear three-button navy blue or black sack suits with cuffs, black shoes, white cotton shirts, and rep or foulard ties. Superficial? Yes, but why jeopardize something as important as accomplishing the mission for something as easily corrected as clothing. Women should dress along the same conservative lines. The president who dresses this way will be accepted in any boardroom, country or university club, or at any social or professional function.

PERCEIVED SELF-CONFIDENCE AND CHARISMA

Perceived self-confidence is another quality of the charismatic leader (Bass, 1981; McClelland, 1976). It is conveyed through comportment, speech, and personal mannerisms, as well as through the decisions the leader makes. While self-confidence implies respect for others, it also conveys an unequivocal strength of purpose and conviction. Effective leaders are so self-confident that they are willing to appoint as close associates those who are superior to them. Usually there is no choice, for leaders need associates on whom they can test and buttress their grand and confident generalizations. Yet wise leaders never lose sight of the fact that they hold the ultimate responsibility.

Charismatic leaders have a positive self-image that grants greater self-confidence. This sense of self-worth engenders respect for others and allows leaders to care deeply about others because they care for themselves. Father Hesburgh writes that "self-confidence enables college presidents to stand alone rather than being drawn into the group" (1979). Self-confidence also allows the leader to maintain social distance and to tolerate the "real loneliness of high position" (Greenleaf, 1977).

Few leaders achieve the image of self-confidence by chance. Bass points out that effective leaders "engage in impression management to bolster their image of confidence, increasing competence, and faith in them" (1985). He also notes that effective leaders are wonderful actors who know that they are always on stage and perform accordingly.

Bennis and Nanus report that effective leaders "don't think about failure, don't even use the word" (1985, p. 70). Whetten and Cameron agree that leaders concentrate on winning, that they have an "innoculation theory" against failure and are less threatened by its prospect (1985).

Great leaders typically are not the most modest people. However, their self-confidence is not based on self-worship, arrogance, or coldness. Indeed, the leader will constantly behave in terms of the best interest of the mission.

OTHER CHARISMATIC INFLUENCES

Other psychological factors may affect charisma. Katz discusses leaders who are charismatic because they become magical symbols of the solutions that followers wish for to solve internal conflicts (1973). Followers can perceive a leader as having attributes that can advance their own particular interests. A defensive charisma not only depends on lofty goals, but continues (or replicates) dependence on a parent. The two conditions necessary for this identification are the parent figure's overwhelming power and the inability of the follower to escape the exercise of that power.

Each of these psychological factors, especially the first two (being perceived as a magical symbol or seeming to advance the interests of the followers), are products of the leader's effective use of distance, style, and perceived self-confidence. They enable the leader to symbolize hope and advance the interests of the people.

DIMINISHING CHARISMA

Charismatic qualities tend to diminish with time. The leadership role becomes increasingly difficult for many reasons. Familiarity with colleagues almost inevitably increases. Most leaders, even those who know better, cannot maintain indefinitely the distance necessary for maximum leadership effectiveness. Time and experience tend to reduce the mystique. As people come to know their leader, they find a reflection of their own doubts, uncertainties, and limitations. Although they like the person more, they admire the leader less and are likely to be less supportive.

It is easier for a leader appointed from outside the organization to develop charismatic qualities than it is for one appointed from within. It follows that outsiders have a better chance of becoming long-tenured leaders. This is not to say that organizations should always go outside for leadership, but unless someone from within is truly exceptional, it's not a bad idea.

While there are a few exceptions, seven to ten years in a particular office is about the maximum term for effectively exerting charismatic power. Contrary to popular belief, the smaller and less complex the organization, the more difficult it is to maintain charisma. People come to know their leader more easily in these situations. While there are noteworthy exceptions to the ten year rule, the wise leader rarely gambles on the odds. Typically, after seven to ten years, the charismatic leader must rely increasingly on expertise, which is not taken as seriously as it was earlier in his or her tenure.

Many leaders who have passed their peak effectiveness tend to rely on legitimate or coercive power instead. In other words, they merely give orders that increasingly may not be obeyed. As a result, they often resign or are forced out of office. This is unfortunate because it compromises their earlier charismatic record. But once charisma is lost or on the wane in a particular setting, regaining it in that setting is almost impossible. The wise leader makes plans to move on before the glow is gone. A charismatic leader can move to another setting and start over again, following one success with another. When the leader has a genuine interest in the next position, he or she can be even more effective.

In sum, charisma is the most significant form of leadership. What the astute leader does, to the extent possible, is gain each of the other leadership forms (expertise, legitimacy, reward, and coercive) and from that base apply the characteristics of charisma. Charisma is developed in the same way a virtuoso plays an instrument—thoughtfully, gently, intelligently, yet enthusiastically.

In the following chapter, the reader will note that the characteristics found in this first systematic study of the effective college president are remarkably similar to the research discussed in this chapter.

Chapter 3

The Effective College President

In 1985, Martha Tack, Karen Wheeler, and I set out to conduct a systematic study of the effective college presidency (Fisher, Tack, and Wheeler, 1988). We were greatly helped in our work by a previous study conducted by George Pruitt (1974). While countless researchers had reported on the model or typical college president and others had written about presidential styles, we were unconvinced that those efforts were a helpful representation of the effective president. Indeed, the contrary might be the case if the average became the standard. Armed with a grant from the Exxon Education Foundation, we directed our three-year study toward *effective* presidents rather than typical presidents. Simply put, we found that the effective president was different from the person normally appointed by a governing board to a college presidency. The effective president appears to be a different kind of person who holds a different kind of leadership philosophy. The effective president is a strong, caring, action-oriented visionary who acts out of educated intuition. A more detailed description of the study can be found in our book, *The Effective College President* (1988).

Initially we identified a cadre of effective college presidents: that group included about 15 percent of the 2,800 presidents included in the research study who were considered by their peers and selected experts as effective. Ninety-five presidents, or approximately 3 percent of those in the sample population, were identified by three or more experts as being effective leaders.

Why do there appear to be relatively few effective presidents in higher education today? We agreed that a number of forces at play make it easier to be a "headman," as Cowley termed it, than to be a leader (1980). In other words, it is easier and safer to keep the lid on things than to stir them up.

These forces include the popular position that truly effective leadership is in effect when consensus consistently reigns (Parks, 1986), when everyone in the organization is happily involved, and when decisions invariably reflect the views of the majority. When consensus reigns, there are no serious problems. Under a consensus condition, how could a generally poor situation be improved? This is a question that addresses the condition of general education today. During the course of more than one hundred consultations, I have found that over-reliance by governing boards and presidents on popular rule and misguided notions about collegiality have led to a dramatic reduction in the ability of the appointed president to lead. Additionally, there had been a significant decline in both institutional morale and effectiveness.

As noted above, a number of writers maintain that the solution to the problems in higher education lies in decision-making based on a consensus born of collegiality (Birnbaum, 1988; Epstein, 1974; Green, 1988; Parks, 1986; Tead, 1951; Walker, 1981). To the contrary, collegial leaders are accepted during periods of relative prosperity, and even then it helps if the institution has a sizable endowment. One president put it this way: "When things get tough, the first one to go is the good collegial president."

In 1988 Davis concluded, "Where the president once was accorded a modicum of differential respect, he/she is now a public figure and fair game for [all]". The position of the college president must be strengthened and restored to some sense of legitimacy if we really expect any positive and lasting advances to be made in post-secondary education (Fisher, 1984; Kerr, 1984; Kerr and Gade, 1986). In this there need be *no compromise* in the historic and important concept of shared governance (see Chapter 6).

To the contrary, according to our research, effective college presidents not only tend to retain final authority and make hard decisions, but they support, praise, challenge, and encourage creativity (even contrary opinion), and are committed to participatory (shared) governance. To a much greater extent than the typical president, the effective president attempts to empower others. Based on these premises, the argument that this is an either/or situation is null. Indeed, during challenging times, others can rarely be empowered without strong leadership.

The history of higher education proves the point. At the fledgling University of Paris, unrestrained faculty power resulted in such chaos that the government finally assumed control. Later at Oxford and Cambridge, only royal courts could sway the senior faculty dominated institutions. Today you need only review a few issues of the *Chronicle of Higher Education* to find features about inviolate faculty interests and an unresponsive curriculum. Brucker concludes that, in the broader corporate world, without exception, every attempt at worker ownership of business over the past 150 years has failed (1988). In higher education, the New School for Social Research in New

York City, which began without a president, was led by a committee of professors. This innovation was temporary. Whatever the problems with the position, presidents do seem to be necessary.

ATTRIBUTES OF EFFECTIVE PRESIDENTS

Our study involved 615 college and university presidents (75 percent of the population surveyed) from two-year, four-year, public, and private institutions. Of this group, 312 respondents were identified by colleagues and qualified observers as being effective in the execution of their presidential responsibilities. The 303 participants who were not nominated were our "representative" chief executive officers. In order to gather data and make comparisons, we used the "Fisher-Tack Effective Leadership Inventory," an instrument developed, pilot-tested, and distributed to the presidents involved. We also interviewed eighteen effective presidents, representing each sector of higher education, to gain additional insight into the intricacies of their leadership.

THE EFFECTIVE COLLEGE PRESIDENT AS A PERSON

Effective college presidents can be described as very *self-confident and positive*. Specifically, effective presidents scored higher on the confidence index (one of five indices included in our instrument) than did representative presidents. Interviews confirmed the tendency of effective presidents to view problems as unrealized opportunities. They focus on success and seem to see the positive side of everything. Because they believe in their ability to make a difference in the world, they tend to work countless hours to achieve their goals. The most highly regarded presidents in America are completely committed to their mission. Unfortunately, they often risk their health as well as their private lives in the process.

While effectiveness and individual self-confidence are inextricably intertwined, *effective college presidents also have a high level of confidence in those with whom they work*. They are positive about the ability of others to make important contributions. They see every member of the campus community—faculty, students, and staff—as capable of making a difference. Effective presidents empower others by believing in them and frequently demonstrating this confidence by making them as autonomous as possible.

Effective presidents demonstrate their confidence by their actions. The connection between risk-taking, courage, and leadership success is well established in the general leadership literature. Effective college presidents are greater *risk-takers* than their representative counterparts. They are not reckless; rather, they tend to act out of informed insight rather than from documented strategic plans. They identify opportunities, analyze the information at hand, consult others, and then make a decision. They are willing to take prudent or calculated risks again and again in order to keep the momentum going.

However, as the people interviewed commented, in taking risks and making decisions, these presidents are not trying to play God. Effective presidents recognize that other people's lives and professions are at stake. They do not want to appear callous or to make decisions without careful consideration. They review all of the variables before deciding which direction they will take. Once the decision is made, they use carefully selected language to convey it to others enthusiastically.

Effective presidents *are strategists who think carefully about what they say and do.* They do not speak extemporaneously as frequently as do their representative counterparts. They do not often engage in verbal exchanges and brainstorming sessions with members of their community. However, they encourage controversy and board discussion.

Time and time again, the eighteen interviewed presidents emphasized that to be effective the president *must have control over his or her emotions, actions, and words.* They seemed to feel that as presidents they were always being observed, perhaps even analyzed, by someone. While in this study no differences emerged in the way presidents approach the management of their "image," effective presidents tend to be more concerned than other presidents about the messages they send to others. In essence, effective presidents believe an "aura" is essential to effective leadership.

EFFECTIVE LEADERSHIP AND THE PRESIDENTIAL POSITION

Effective presidents respect, but *do not feel bound by administrative structure as others might.* While they tend to believe that there should be a hierarchy and a chain of command to facilitate the smooth operation of the institution, they refuse to be boxed in by organizational constraints. Those who work with such leaders soon learn that these presidents are likely to appear anywhere at any time.

How do these presidents feel about their institutions? In addition to being committed to their work (in fact, it is so often difficult to distinguish the presidency from the person), the effective presidents *believe more strongly in the mission than in the institution itself.* They tend to candidly define the institution in terms of the mission.

Effective presidents *value strategic and long-range planning, but they clearly believe more strongly in the power of ideas and vision.* While they work very hard to see that their colleges and universities succeed, both in terms of a high-quality academic reputation and responsiveness to societal needs, effective presidents tend to see their institutions as part of a larger society with broader goals. For these individuals, the dream of what might be is always alive; their institutions are vehicles for achieving this dream. In fact, in this context, they sometimes make decisions that are not in the immediate best interest of their respective institutions.

THE EFFECTIVE COLLEGE PRESIDENT AND SOCIAL RELATIONSHIPS

When we looked at the human relations aspect of leadership, we found no overt differences in presidential behaviors. That is, possessing finely honed human relations skills is a generic attribute of most presidents. However, in social situations, the way that effective college presidents relate to and think about others is dramatically different from that of representative chief executive officers.

As noted previously, self-confidence and risk-taking seem essential to successful leadership. Therefore, it should come as no surprise that, when compared to their representative counterparts, *effective presidents are more likely to believe that respect is more important than collegiality or popularity.* This is clearly consistent with McClelland and Burnham's research in the broader leadership arena, in which they conclude that effective leaders are more concerned with results than with either affiliation or personal recognition (1976).

This critical attitudinal difference exists because of the interactive nature of these important attributes, commitment to a lofty goal, an overwhelmingly clear vision for the future, competence, and the leader's confidence in his or her ability to lead. Father Theodore Hesburgh, President Emeritus of Notre Dame and the most frequently named effective president, says, "Leadership is . . . not for one requiring praise and moral support. The leader gives these; he or she cannot count on getting them. The leader's task is to realize the vision in its totally; his or her reward is to see that happen" (1988).

While both effective and representative presidents respect the rights and opinions of others, effective presidents are more inclined to encourage staff and faculty to take risks, to think differently, to be creative, and to share their thoughts, no matter how diverse. Effective presidents seem willing to meet almost any test in the conviction that their vision will be enhanced. Moreover, these presidents try to surround themselves with exceedingly able people who are futurists, often different by conventional standards; and they actively solicit input from constituents. In support of this idea, the interviewed presidents are more prone to support and encourage creative and reflective thought, even though they know these ideas may be in conflict with their own views. They are willing to take a more tortuous course and to make controversial decisions, because they believe that broad community respect and support can be achieved through this process.

Completely contrary to conventional wisdom in higher education, effective presidents are not as constrained by consensus when making decisions as are representative presidents. Indeed, the effective presidents we interviewed believe less in the importance of trying to achieve consensus than do all of the other chief executive officers we studied. In no way does this finding suggest that effective presidents exist in isolation; rather, they actively seek input from those who will be directly affected by the decision. They encourage the creation of mechanisms to provide this input. Effective presidents will make the hard decisions and, if need be, move against the winds of consensus, always trying to regain support.

A good example of the willingness of effective presidents to move against the mainstream is their support for the controversial idea of merit pay. Effective presidents believe more strongly in this concept than do those in the representative group. While effective presidents tend to agree that money is not really a primary motivator, they recognize the importance of communicating to those who are the most productive that their efforts are appreciated. While most believe merit pay to be too subjective and controversial, effective presidents are more willing to take a stand on measuring an elusive excellence. They often campaign actively for the recognition of meritorious service.

These presidents are willing to make hard decisions, risk momentary disfavor, and move forward because of one key attitude: as presidents, they do not believe in close collegial relationships to the extent that representative presidents do. Most effective presidents believe it to be virtually impossible to have intimate friendships with those they would lead. We speculate that this is because of the constraints such friendships can place on the leader's ability to make, or to be perceived as making, unbiased decisions.

Presidents need to maintain social and psychological distance in order to enhance respect and appreciation. While honest debate is essential, familiarity breeds unproductive discussions. Effective leaders balance distance and privacy with closeness and familiarity. They lead warmly, with care and respect, but always from their presidential positions. As long as they are presidents, they do not try to pretend they are not.

Effective presidents use their positions with finesse. They are not as driven by the desire for personal recognition or popularity, nor are they bent on being kings or queens. Rather, they have their sights set on greater goals and work as intelligently as they can in order to achieve them. While their leadership behaviors and attitudes may sometimes be misunderstood, they are almost invariably respected.

Interviewed presidents said that they are genuinely concerned about the welfare of those with whom they work, but they believe they must be willing to say "no" if the greater goals are to be served. Nonetheless, effective presidents also tend to believe that when they have to use their presidential power to compel people to do something, they lose a part of their ability to lead effectively. Therefore, they make every effort to achieve support and to depersonalize decisions.

Effective presidents also believed strongly that they should often be out front and visible and that, in all but a few institutions, presidential visibility is necessary to advance the cause. These same presidents believe fervently in sharing the credit for success with others, including staff and faculty.

In summary, these high-profile college presidents appear to be more confident and more willing to take risks, even when their personal welfare is involved. They are distant rather than collegial; they rarely speak spontaneously; and they make hard, often controversial, decisions. Yet they have a profound respect for and appreciation of the role of others (including faculty) in decision-making. They have a greater sense of where higher education fits in the scheme of things, and they are able to represent their goals and values effectively (and they repeat them frequently before all constituencies). Their lofty aspirations for the enterprise and for their institutions push them to accomplish their goals. They feel that they are competent managers, intuitive decision-makers, and entrepreneurs.

IMPLICATIONS

The implications of this study should be particularly important to governing boards, as well as to those who are or would be presidents.

As Kerr's study concluded, too often the person selected to serve as the college president is the one to whom no one strongly objects (1984). This is a sad commentary about the way we select the people who are to lead our institutions. The following chapter discusses how boards can exercise their responsibilities more thoughtfully and strongly in the presidential appointment process. Contrary to prevailing opinion, the process needs to be closed rather than open. Board members should take a more active role, "shops" should be put in order, and the whole process made more efficient and consistent with the appointment of potentially effective leaders.

Chapters 5-Chapter 9 apply the same strong critical assessment to the general condition of many institutions, particularly college and university governance and presidential evaluation. Today, this condition is often an unfortunate by-product of an erosion of the structure of our society and the reduced legitimacy of our leaders who are held responsible but are too often essentially unempowered. In higher education, these conditions can only be remedied by thoughtful governing boards.

Each of the following chapters considers the role and relationship of the board and the president from the premises of the research on effective leadership presented in the preceding two chapters. The reader should bear in mind that all of the recommendations made are in keeping with the letter and spirit of the 1940 and 1966 AAUP statements on academic freedom and on government.

Chapter 4

The Presidential Search Process

It is ironic that as the presidential search process has become increasingly sophisticated, the presidency itself has become the major dilemma in higher education. Harvard's David Riesman has referred to today's presidential search as "the search and destroy process." Scholars and national associations are candid about the issue. It is now well established that presidential leadership is the main imperative for the revitalization of higher education. Certainly no commission or study group has concluded that the search process is the prime culprit in the decline of the presidency; rather it is only another symptom, although an extremely important one, of the leadership dilemma in higher education. It is the thesis of this chapter that the presidential search process is the unfortunate beginning of the compromised presidency in American higher education.

The presidential selection process was an early victim of the new existential order. In strong spirit and without effective dissent, presidential selection became popularized. As faculty members and students achieved closer and formal ties with governing boards, gradually both the process and the result of presidential appointment changed. The process of presidential selection became more important than the outcome. Increasingly, the weight of "the people" was felt in the process of presidential selection, and the presidency got lost in the democratic shuffle. Presidents could not safely object to the new order; they either hoped it would work or silently rode the tide.

Strong candidates and confidentiality automatically fell by the wayside as the sunshine of open meetings and participation shone on the campus and in the media. At this writing, sixteen states have open meeting "sunshine" laws requiring that all presidential search meetings for public institutions be open to the public. Top people became increasingly reluctant to be candidates. Those who did either dropped out because of the threat (or certainty) of breaching confidentiality, or were eliminated by zealous faculty-dominated search committees looking for signs of controversy. Governing boards scarcely noticed as their institutional incline turned downward. Left with neither rational form nor order, presidents came and went or quietly sat on the bench while boards and faculties tried to run the institutions.

A FLAWED SEARCH PROCESS

The compromise of presidential legitimacy begins, and in too many cases continues, with the presidential appointment process. If the first steps in this crucial process are unwise, regardless of outside counsel and the most sophisticated material, the outcome will be mediocre. Indeed, if a good candidate happens to slip through, it will be by accident rather than by sound intention. The institution will most likely end up with one of those "faceless" presidents who reportedly characterize higher education today, it will drift or get into serious trouble.

In most institutions today, the search process is fundamentally flawed. Either a good committee is doing the wrong things, or a poorly constituted committee is doing the right things. In either case, the next president is a compromise.

In the first case, the typical reconstituted search committee pools its inexperience and establishes a "new" procedure. *A poor process is the result.* The committee tends to focus on the process rather than the outcome, attempting to involve virtually all interested parties. These committees often do such questionable things as create additional faculty and even administration committees, cater to the media, take too long to get the job done, design committee stationery, invite the outgoing president to join them, appoint too many faculty members to the search committee (or too few board members), appoint a faculty/student screening committee, assign a faculty member to handle the administration of committee matters, hold public interviews with final candidates, appoint all sorts of advisory and subcommittees, and, most unfortunately, they decide that they can do the job without outside consultation.

In the second case, a poor search committee includes a disproportionate number of faculty, members of the administrative staff, and board members who don't realize that no board responsibility is more important than the appointment of a president.

Occasionally, top candidates do survive this happy egalitarian process. This, plus a pleased search committee, is enough to lull a governing board into acceptance, at least initially. In time, as the governing board becomes too involved in campus administration and external relations, it begins to question the president, all the while forgetting that its problems started with the presidential search process.

What *should* a board do when there is a presidential vacancy? This chapter describes a tested presidential search procedure, fashioned after careful review of the research on effective leadership.

WHAT THE BOARD SHOULD NOT DO WITH A PRESIDENTIAL VACANCY

Let us assume that you are the board chair and your president has just informed you of his intention to leave office in fifteen months. What is the first step? You should *not* convene the board and appoint a search committee. In most instances, a presidential vacancy prompts a review of what was done previously; old minutes are reviewed, and "new" procedures are really "old-fashioned" revivals. After all, who could get into trouble in this most sensitive and important area by following precedent? The answer is, almost everybody.

The ignorance of the past is given new life by a well-intentioned board that does not know what else to do. A mistake made in the appointment of the search committee is usually irreparable.

The key features in an efficient and effective presidential search are: (1) the use of more outside consultants than you think you will need; (2) the right search committee; (3) the right search process; (4) complete confidentiality; (5) an institutional review or audit; (6) an emphasis on referencing rather than interviewing; and (7) a finely tailored compensation package.

WHAT THE BOARD SHOULD DO

The following five steps should take approximately two weeks. (Weeks 1 and 2)

(1) The Appointment of a General Consultant

After it has been ensured that the ongoing president will have a graceful departure, the single most important thing that a board can do is to engage an experienced general consultant. It should do this before anything else— that is, *before appointing a search committee*. After discussions with the chair of the board, the consultant should speak to a meeting of the full board or the executive committee.

A prestigious middle-Atlantic university was prepared to appoint a seventeen member faculty screening committee who would review all candidates before they were reviewed by a board search committee. The board chair was prepared to do this even after acknowledging that the same screening committee process had produced a president who lasted an unhappy four years. After outside consultation, the committee immediately changed course. The chair changed the design and involved the faculty in a way that was helpful yet not compromising to the search.

At this point, you don't need a search consultant. Rather, you need someone who is broadly experienced in higher education, a scholar and/or a successful CEO. This consultant should speak about the general condition and future prospects of higher education, particularly as related to institutions similar to yours; review recent research on the college presidency; and discuss the presidential appointment process, placing special emphasis on your search for a new president.

(2) The Appointment of the Search Committee

The general consultant should advise you about whom to appoint to your search committee. In most cases, *it is absolutely vital that you hear from your consultant (or read this) before appointing the search committee.* Most institutions appoint the search committee first, and by the time they hear from the consultant, it is too late. The selection process is already hostage to a committee heavily loaded with faculty as well as staff and students; ergo, the politics of the campus has infected and probably contaminated the search process. The committee should consider the various vested interests of the campus community, but those interests should not be heavily represented on the search committee.

This is what too often happens:

I once served as a consultant for the presidential search committee of an eastern liberal arts college. The committee of thirteen (too many) included four trustees, four faculty members, three administrators, and two students. They asked me to advise them about a selection procedure that would result in a wise choice. After a day and a half during which we established a candid rapport, they finally agreed that regardless of what process they followed, they were certain to make a less than desirable presidential choice. They realized that even if they followed the most sophisticated presidential selection procedures and used the most astute consultants, they were bound to appoint the wrong person. The reason being that with the exception of the trustees (who were outnumbered), this was a political committee, each faculty, staff, and student tacitly but finally obligated to a particular vested interest within the college. With one vote, they were bound to end up with a compromise candidate, a negotiator, a manager, the average rather than the exception. In spite of initial protestations to the contrary, they finally concluded that, while they might all be involved in the presidential appointment process in some other way, the college would be best served if their search committee was dissolved, and it was.

There are two ways to minimize the politicization of your search committee: (1) adhere strictly to the message of the research on effective management and leadership, which clearly calls for *no* representative of members of the community on the search committee (that is, no faculty senate representative, no one elected or appointed by anyone except the governing board); or (2) appoint a committee with a distinct majority of strong trustee members and only modest representation from the campus community. In higher education, the second is probably the wisest choice. However, according to a survey by David Riesman and Judith McLaughlin on search committee composition, more than 50 percent of the institutions surveyed reported that "less than one-half" of their search committee members were trustees; and 16 percent reported that *no* trustees served on their search committee (Riesman and McLaughlin, 1984).

The general consultant may advise you to opt for the second example, a committee composed largely of trustees. Regardless of institutional politics, the ideal size for such a search committee is nine (but never fewer than seven or more than fifteen): five strong trustees, two faculty members, one student, and one alumnus. As chair of the board, you should also chair the search committee. If you choose not to be chair yourself, appoint (never elect) your strongest board member.

Notice that there are no administrators on the committee. Administrators are members of the president's team, and no candidate should be given the impression that the administration plays a role in selecting the president. The leadership research also indicates that committee members should not be chosen by institution-wide election. If the faculty governance body is asked to name four or five faculty representatives, they may choose to elect them. While it would be better if faculty spokespersons were appointed by their council, let *them* choose how they will do it. This issue is not worth a disagreement with the faculty as long as board members constitute a majority of the search committee.

After you decide on committee membership, ask the chief academic officer or the interim president (*not* the outgoing president) to act as your agent in discussions about how the faculty will choose their representatives. This will allow you to maintain the necessary distance between the board and the faculty and will not threaten the leadership of your next president. Remember, close that gap and you risk leaving out your president in other things after the appointment. Always, but always, play up the presidential office. In the long run, it will make things run smoothly and easily.

In most situations, in order to satisfy faculty expectations the chief academic officer or interim president should also ask the primary faculty governance body to appoint a special committee of faculty; one from each school, college, or division and, perhaps, a student and an alumnus. Toward the end of the presidential search, this committee would be asked to interview *in complete confidence* the top choices of the search committee. Bear in mind that faculty members are as trustworthy as corporate executives. Each member of this advisory committee would then evaluate the candidates on a special form prepared by your consultant. At the conclusion of the candidate interviews, the assigned chair (usually one of the faculty members of the search committee) collects the forms without discussion and gives them to you to share with the full board as it makes the final decision.

(3) Committee Staff

You need to appoint a loyal, discreet staff member who will serve as the administrative officer and secretary for the search committee. This person takes notes, makes meeting arrangements, staffs the search office, handles correspondence, maintains files, and provides other services to the committee. He or she does not vote or, except in an objective role, participate in the discussions of the committee.

After talking with the general consultant, have the news office on campus prepare a press release announcing the general time frame (two months to a year is acceptable, but four to six months is best) and stressing the confidentiality of the search. You should also make it clear that all future comments on the search process will come either from you or from the chair of the search committee.

(4) Confidentiality

Confidentiality *cannot* be overemphasized. More good candidates are lost or are never attracted because of a lack of confidentiality than for all other reasons combined. This is particularly true of states with sunshine laws but it happens in others as well. Confidentiality means confidential *to the end*. Many believe that the final stages of the process should include public interviews on campus. The idea is without foundation. Not only are good candidates lost in this way, but personal interviews, including public interviews, are the *least* effective variable in predicting job success. The key to your best candidates will be the institutional review and careful referencing by the committee and the consultant. Interviews have gained currency in higher education simply because of a kind of politics vested in collegiality and, because governing boards do not know what else to do.

(5) Charge to the Search Committee

The next step is preparing a board charge to the search committee. (Appendix A) This charge will probably include, among other things, a statement about the departing president, the names of the search committee members, the general time frame of the search, and how many candidates should be recommended (three to five in *no* order of preference). The charge should emphasize again the importance of confidentiality (see appendices).

The board should approve all of the appropriate conditions. Now you are ready for the first meeting of the committee.

(6) The First Meeting of the Search Committee (Week 3)

(See Appendix B for a concise step-by-step process of a four-month search.)

The first meeting should be brief, instructive, and carefully planned. The agenda should approximate the following:

    1. opening remarks by the chair;
    2. presentation by general consultant;
** 3. consideration of search consultants;
** 4. consideration of institutional audit or review;
** 5. consideration of compensation study;
    6. consideration of specific time frame;
    7. consideration of public hearing;
** 8. ads: design and posting;
** 9. special letters;
  10. presentation by outgoing president;
  11. presentation by affirmative action officer;
** 12. office space, secretary, correspondence;
  13. other matters.

**Some boards have found it helpful to determine these things *prior* to the first meeting of the search committee.

Your opening remarks (item 1) should be brief but inspiring. Don't assume that committee members recognize the profound importance of their task. After everyone takes a blood oath to confidentiality, read the board's charge to the committee, review the agenda, and then proceed.

Next on your agenda is a presentation by the general consultant (item 2). It should include a review of the condition of higher education, specifically that of the presidency; a review of the research on effective leadership, emphasizing the college presidency; a presentation of a generic search process; and then a discussion of items three through seven on the agenda. Committee members should be invited to ask questions.

The third item on your agenda calls for a consideration of search consultants. (It is perfectly acceptable for you to appoint a search consultant before the first committee meeting; just be sure to discuss this with the general consultant first.) Although there may be institutions whose trustees and staff are sufficiently involved and informed to be sophisticated about presidential search, I have never known of any. You should avoid, at all costs, the common tendency to dig out old files and personnel (board or staff) who have participated in past searches. If you want to do the best job possible, you *must* appoint an outside search consultant. This is true for state systems as well, even those who have full-time officers assigned to conduct searches. Increasingly, boards of trustees agree as more and more appoint search consultants to help in this fundamental task. Good search consultants know both the process of presidential searches and the universe of prospective presidents. They also have their reputations on the line each time they accept an assignment.

To choose a search firm from the variety of possibilities, make a few calls, but always interview at least three prospects. The general consultant can provide the names of top search firms and can help monitor the work of the one you select.

There are two basic kinds of search firms, not-for-profit and profit. Using either kind is better than doing the search yourself. The not-for-profit firms have been criticized for concentrating too much on the search *process*. While they seem to invariably leave the people involved happy, some feel they should focus more on the project at hand, the appointment of the best possible president. Although nonprofit firms usually take longer to do the job, their fees are generally lower.

The for-profit firms are more concerned with outcome, take less time (four to six months), and charge more (usually a third of the first year's salary). Both the profit and the nonprofit firms are sometimes faulted for a lack of substantive knowledge of and experience with effective leadership in universities and colleges. There is also concern, largely unsubstantiated, that these firms draw on a common pool of candidates for all institutions and that they will accept without enlightened critique any design for a search, so long as they win the contract.

Through the years, in my role as a general consultant to governing boards and search committees, I have probably heard more presentations by more search firms than anyone else in the country. I have yet to be completely satisfied with any. Virtually none are thoughtful students of issues in higher education or effective leadership, and few are represented by former successful college presidents. It is only natural that they tend to represent the parochial interests of the search committee rather than providing the committee with objective information that may be valuable in forming the board or committee members' impressions and enabling them to make decisions. This said, however, bear in mind that using these firms is infinitely better than doing the search yourself (even with this book in hand) because of their higher efficiency and greater knowledge of the candidates in the field.

I tend to lean towards the for-profit firms because most are more goal-oriented, but many boards have been completely happy with the nonprofit firms and have saved themselves several thousand dollars in the process.

Whatever you do, stay in touch with the process; you will feel better and keep your consultant alert. It is not at all unusual for a search committee chair to talk with the search consultant three to six times a week.

If you decide to use a search consultant, the following may be helpful: before you invite the search firm representatives for an interview, the general consultant presents a brief on each firm. If you interview three firms, at least one should be not-for-profit. Your general consultant can recommend a number of highly regarded profit and nonprofit firms. You and the committee members may wish to add to this list.

The most important consideration here is that you check references on each firm. You and your associates on the committee should feel good about the person making the presentation. You should also make sure that the persons doing the presentation will be assigned by the firm to do this search. In the past, boards and search committees have been known to sign contracts under the belief that they would be working with the person who made such a powerful presentation, only to find later that another person is assigned to do the job.

After introductions, ask the representative of the firm to make a brief presentation (no more than twenty minutes) and then to answer questions from the committee. Here are some questions you may want to consider:

How long will it take to do a thorough search?

What do you think of our institution?

What experience have you had with similar institutions?

What kind of president do you think we need?

What role will we, the committee, play in the search process?

How do you reference candidates? Do we help?

Why shouldn't we do this ourselves?

What do you, or others in your firm, know about higher education?

Are any members of your firm former college presidents?

Are you associated with any scholars in higher education?

Do you do a reading of the campus before focusing on candidates?

If so, how? Tell us more about the process.

How many searches do you conduct simultaneously?

Should faculty be represented on a search committee? Should students be represented? If so, how heavily?

How do you feel about the use of screening and advisory committees to assist the search committee?

Is confidentiality really important? If so, how is it maintained?
What about public interviews?
What is the difference between a profit and a nonprofit search firm?
Why do you ask us to pay your fee in installments?

After all of the presentations, the committee should discuss the firms with the general consultant and then make its selection. From this point on, the search firm is your primary instrument in the search process. However, you should continue to involve the general consultant as your surrogate. You will need to decide the extent to which he or she will be involved. In some instances, telephone contact is sufficient; in others, the general consultant continues to attend all committee meetings to closely advise on procedures, the institutional review, media and public relations, and to review the activities of the search consultant. *Whatever you do, let the search firm know that the general consultant will review the files of all candidates. It helps keep them honest.*

The fourth item is the institutional audit or review. Many boards (e.g., the University of North Carolina at Chapel Hill) have found of indispensable value an institutional audit or review conducted by the general consultant or by another person from outside the institution who is considered an authority (see Chapter 5). The decision to conduct an audit may also be made prior to the appointment of a search committee. This commissioned consultant appoints a review team of four to six people of stature. Through interviews, campus visits, and reading materials, the team reviews all areas of the institution (academic programs, faculty, students, administration, budget, finances, fund raising, public relations, and governance) and presents you with a written report. The report can be either confidential or public, but most would agree that the report is more valuable when made public. This review is the basis for both a profile of and a tentative agenda for the next president.

If the report is made public, it will receive wide publicity, and virtually all interested parties, both on-campus and off-campus, will be sensitized to the problems and the prospects for the new president, and all will be more enthusiastic about the institution and the board. Boards have also found these institutional reviews helpful in stirring the interests of top presidential candidates and in conducting interviews with finalists in the search process. Indeed, some leading candidates, including finalists, have not been interested until they have read the institutional review. A thorough review can take from eight to ten weeks. Commission it early so it will be of maximum value in the search process.

If the board has not already commissioned one, the fifth item on your agenda calls for considering the need for a presidential compensation study (more on this in Chapter 8). If your outgoing president has been in office five or more years and has not had an outside compensation study, you need one badly. Some searches have broken down at the end because the board has taken for granted the subject of presidential compensation or has assumed the validity of ancient conditions. One state institution recently lost its first-choice candidate because its presidential housing allowance was $6,000 per year (a board policy from 1967), and the board could not get a policy change approved by the state in time to keep the candidate. Other institutions have lost attractive candidates who say nothing, but are turned off when they learn of the compensation package.

If you are in doubt about your compensation package, have a good executive compensation firm run a two-phase study, the first to study your opening package, and the second to develop a defined package tailored to the needs and the situation of your final choice. Indeed, this could just be the clincher for a top candidate. It demonstrates that you are thoughtful, and it provides the kind of security a president needs but rarely mentions. Whatever you do about compensation, think about it seriously and specifically in advance.

Your time frame (item 6) will usually be around a year, but a thorough search should be conducted in much less time. The average search takes approximately seven and one-half months, and you can do a better job if you do it in less time, never more. Too much time makes for a sloppy search in which the task of finding a top president runs a greater risk of becoming obscured by politics and breaching confidentiality. A number of boards have found it wise to publicly announce a longer time period but to shoot for less. This will get better results and more readily lull the media and other pressing interests into your confidential design. Whatever the time frame, it should be broken down into four sections: (1) promotion; (2) review; (3) interviews; and (4) recommendations.

Unless it has already been established by the board, another matter on the first meeting agenda should be the consideration of a public hearing (item 7) on the appropriate characteristics of the next president. This hearing should take place on the campus and all potentially interested parties should be invited, by letter and through the public media, to register *in advance* (Appendix C). As many members of the search committee as possible should sit quietly on the panel, which is presided over by the committee chair. It is generally unwise for committee members to engage in dialogue with presenters or others in the audience. The purpose of these meetings is to encourage all interested parties to advise the committee. The chair announces the rules, and the meeting continues until all presenters have spoken. The secretary of the search committee is present, and the entire proceedings are taped for future reference. This practice serves two purposes: the committee has the advantage of additional insights, and the members of the community and others have the opportunity to become significantly involved in the search for a new leader.

The promotional period includes placing ads (item 8) in the *Chronicle of Higher Education* and the *New York Times*, in major regional newspapers in your area, and in major special-interest publications for minorities and women. Put the ads in quickly and run them for at least one month. You can also do this before the search committee is appointed. Although this should not be publicly stated, never officially close a search until a final candidate is signed up.

You do not, I repeat, *do not* need to be overly specific in your ads and announcements. Many committees labor over the wording of newspaper and journal ads that are rarely read in detail or taken seriously even by the most interested candidates. This takes up an inordinate amount of time and delays the posting of your vacancy. All you want to do at this stage is get the word out that your presidency is open (Appendix D).

Your consultant will present a suggested list of persons, organizations, and groups who should be invited to submit nominations for the presidency (Appendix E). The committee should send a letter to these persons (and the committee may wish to add others): all college presidents in the region or state; presidents of the same type of institution; presidents of impressive national reputation; key figures in higher education in the state and nation; scholars on the presidency; and the presidents of important national associations in higher education.

Later, you should send this group another letter, inviting additional nominations and containing a copy of the institutional review. Frequently, the institutional review will inspire application of additional top candidates.

At this first meeting, the committee should approve a letter inviting members of the university community, including faculty, staff, students, and alumni, to submit nominations (Appendix F). The letter should be included in campus and alumni publications. Remember, you cannot do too much in inviting interested parties to submit nominations.

Unless the outgoing president is leaving with bad feelings, he or she should be invited to prepare a paper on the condition of the institution (item 10) to present to the full committee. At the close of the president's remarks (no more than thirty minutes), encourage committee members to ask questions. Finally, after no more than fifty minutes, the president should be excused from the meeting, never to be heard from again (unless a specific instance arises where he or she can provide helpful information; then the president can be invited back or interviewed by an assigned member of the committee). Too many search committees muddy their efforts by either inviting the outgoing president to sit on the committee or by snubbing the president altogether by not inviting him or her to make a presentation. I recently heard the chair of a search committee, an otherwise able man, say to the assembled committee in the presence of the incumbent president, "Bill will sit with us for a few meetings, but he has no intention of naming his successor." Talk about an uncomfortable oxymoron.

After the president speaks and is thanked and excused, the members of the committee can feel completely free to speak about anything concerning the institution, including the outgoing president.

Next, the affirmative action officer makes a presentation (item 11). It is important that the committee be sensitized to and informed about the importance of affirmative action considerations. No matter how enlightened the committee may be, this presentation should be made by a staff member who is especially well-informed on the subject. He or she usually has the title "affirmative action officer" and can advise the committee as to the conditions on campus, the law, and sources of good candidates.

After selecting a search consultant, consider any additional matters the committee may wish to raise (such as office space, secretarial help, etc.) and adjourn the meeting.

At this point, the efficient search committee now has three meetings in order to complete its task. During the interim before the second meeting of the committee, nominations and applications begin to arrive. Each candidate should receive a letter of acknowledgment on discrete letterhead, requesting him or her to list three to six references (Appendix G & H). During this period, the consultant does a preliminary sort and selects those candidates who most nearly meet the criteria for the position. This number is usually between thirty and forty. Members of the committee are encouraged to come to the search committee office and evaluate all applications and review correspondence. It is best not to allow anyone, except the consultant, to take candidate files out of the search office. During this period thank you letters should be sent to nominators, applicants and other candidates (Appendix I, J, K).

The institutional review should be completed during this period, and committee members will have had time to assess reactions. The search committee secretary should collect all media comments and provide copies for the next meeting. The consultant should prepare a candidate interview form consistent with the needs documented in the review. You should hold the public hearing the day before the second search committee meeting, with as many search committee members as possible in attendance.

THE SECOND SEARCH COMMITTEE MEETING

Suggested agenda:

1. opening remarks by the chair;
2. review by chair and consultant (stress confidentiality);
3. discussion of institutional review;
4. committee reviews file of top thirty candidates (allow one and one-half to two hours);

5. committee and consultant discuss candidates and reduce list to fifteen to twenty;

6. committee members receive reference assignments (they will use interview forms developed from the institutional review).

The chair opens the meeting (item 1) by stressing confidentiality, the consultant presents a report on activities since the last meeting, including the results of the institutional review.

The chair explains that the consultant has been asked to pare down the candidate group to between thirty and forty (item 2). (Committee members were asked to visit the search office and review all of the candidate files before this meeting.) The committee spends ninety minutes or so reviewing and evaluating candidate files. After asking the committee for additional names (and usually getting none), the chair asks the consultant to lead discussion on the top thirty to forty candidates.

This discussion reduces the list to between fifteen to twenty, and members of the committee are assigned to reference certain candidates, using a form prepared by the consultant from the findings of the institutional review (item 3). The consultant and the committee chair will do in-depth referencing of all candidates. This means going beyond the references provided by the candidates. This is when consultants with board experience in higher education can be of great value through the personal relationships they have formed over the years.

During the interim period preceding the third search committee meeting, the committee and the consultant are engaged in referencing, and the consultant continues developing prospects. The institutional review invariably heightens the interest of the top candidates as well as evoking the interest of new people. For this to happen, you must have sent the institutional review to persons in strategic positions in higher education (Appendix L, M).

THE THIRD SEARCH COMMITTEE MEETING

Suggested agenda:

1. opening remarks by the chair (stress confidentiality);

2. consultant's review of new candidates and prospects, update on others;

3. discuss referencing on remaining fifteen to twenty candidates;

4. reduce list to seven to ten candidates to be reviewed (preferably out of the area); and

5. other business.

During the interim before the fourth and final meeting of the search committee, the committee and the consultant continue referencing. If deemed necessary, site visits may be conducted with the knowledge of the candidate. During any site visits, confidentiality is essential. If such visits are considered necessary—and they are not as valuable as most search committees believe—the consultant should make the visit. Referencing three or four times removed plus the consultant's contacts provide by far the most valuable considerations in the decision-making of the committee. Site visits usually result in more show than substance, but if you need show, and some committees do, make the visits. Just do them carefully.

THE FOURTH SEARCH COMMITTEE MEETING

Schedule this out-of-the-area meeting in a high-quality hotel of sufficient size that candidates to be interviewed are not likely to encounter one another. Arrange specific times for the interviews and tell candidates that they will be called in their rooms regarding where to join the committee.

Suggested agenda:

1. opening remarks by the chair (stress confidentiality);
2. review by consultant;
3. candidate interviews (approximately fifty minutes each);
4. reduce list to three to five candidates to be recommended without preference to the board.

The committee interviews the candidates referenced since the last meeting. Occasionally a reference eliminates a candidate, and infrequently additional candidates are found.

Candidate interviews follow the same format as the one used in referencing. If you assign a specific item of the interview to each member of the search committee, you will ensure that all interviewees are asked essentially the same questions. This will make comparisons easier during the committee discussion following the interviews. The consultant can be sure that all areas are covered in each interview. The chair should welcome the candidate and ask the first question, a fairly easy one to get things off to a smooth start, "Please tell us something about yourself, where you were born, your family, schools, and your career." After that, the committee can ask other questions, both planned and spontaneous. A good interview may take more than fifty minutes.

In the discussion of the candidates, it is important that the committee finally agree on all the candidates to be recommended to the board—that is, the committee must pledge itself to support enthusiastically any of the candidates selected by the board. You may sense which candidates are the first, second, and third choices, but don't rank them.

FINAL INTERVIEWS BY THE BOARD

We are now back at the beginning, with the board about to exercise its most important responsibility, the appointment of the next president. If you are being pressed to hold public campus interviews, don't do it! This is exactly the point when searches have broken down and many candidates have withdrawn. Confidentiality is impossible under such conditions. What you can do instead, if you've done things astutely, is ask the chief academic officer (or the acting president) to invite the faculty senate (or whatever it is called on your campus) to name one faculty member from each unit of the institution to serve on a nonprotein, completely confidential committee that will interview the final candidates. The faculty will have input, and you have maintained confidentiality. You may also invite the student government organization and the alumni association to each name a representative. Ask a faculty member of the search committee to chair this special meeting and, after you have given the committee a brief orientation, leave them to their interviews. Ask this committee not to reach a consensus on each candidate, but to have each member independently fill out the candidate interview form used by the search committee. At the close of the committee meeting, the chair should bring the forms to you where the board is meeting so that the board can consider the reactions of the faculty committee before making its final choice.

You should stagger the interviews so that each candidate is interviewed by the faculty committee before he or she appears before the board. This will test the stamina of the candidate as well as giving the board the benefit of the impressions of the faculty committee before it makes its final decision.

The board interview should follow the same format as that used by the search committee in the first set of interviews. After your initial question, board members from the search committee can take the lead. Once the interview is underway, it should take no more than sixty minutes. Ask the candidate for questions, thank him or her, and say that you will be in touch.

At this stage, observe everything about the candidate: language, presence, dress, posture, eating or drinking habits. But most of all, remember that the personal interview is the *least* valuable predictor of job success; the most important is the referencing that has already been done by your committee and the consultant.

After the interviews, rank your acceptable candidates. Get to your first choice as quickly as possible, but until a contract is signed don't dismiss any candidate. Sophisticated candidates know that a board usually moves quickly after final interviews, and if too much time passes, the uncontacted finalists will withdraw to save face, and you could find yourself in an awkward situation.

Be prepared to offer your top choice precise terms. Have a compensation package prepared well in advance (see Chapter 8); you can lose precious time and even your best candidates toward the end if your package is not sufficient to acquire your choice. It is at this point that you should begin to think seriously about the spouse of your candidate. Spousal happiness is important, and you should consider everything from household appointments and services to employment prospects. (It is generally much better to find the spouse a job off campus than to expect him or her to be a full job partner with the president. Chapter 8 further considers this important subject.)

Once you have your president signed, make the public announcement as soon as possible. This not only lets the public know the final selection but it more seriously ties in the candidate, now the president-elect. Ask the candidate to approve the press release and any plans for a news conference. This is really the beginning of his or her presidency.

Next, inform all other candidates, on the same day the announcement is made. If possible, close and store the files and have the finance records audited. Because you have gone about the process the right way, you have a new president who will bring increased distinction and status to your institution.

Have a party for the committee.

Chapter 5

The Institutional Evaluation (Review)

Increasingly, governing boards are commissioning institutional evaluations (called "reviews" because this term is less perjorative) as a first step toward establishing or re-establishing a solid foundation for the institution and more legitimate premises for the president. Boards and search committees often find these reviews indispensable during presidential searches. Presidents, particularly newly appointed presidents, find that institutional reviews can help them start their presidencies on a solid footing. Sitting presidents have found them useful in finding out "how things really are" and in making future plans. Indeed, institutional reviews are often considered of greater value and validity than accreditation reports, which are sometimes merely exercises in back-scratching or efforts to check the behavior of the unconventional.

WHAT IS AN INSTITUTIONAL REVIEW?

An institutional review is an evaluation of the entire institution, with special attention directed toward strategic positioning.

An institutional review is conducted by a team of outside recognized authorities who, over a two to four month period, assess the condition of an institution through interviews and data. The review is finally presented to the board and/or the president, and it may be used as either a public or a confidential document, although certain benefits are lost in a confidential review. A public review invariably serves as a tonic for the entire institution. Initially, some in the campus community are skeptical, believing that no outsider could really know them; others may be anxious at the thought of discovery; but most are pleased at the prospect of an objective evaluation that could verify their worth and improve their condition. A good review will

59

always meet the test of all concerned parties, including those who were initially skeptical.

The review evaluates every dimension of the institution. The final report should include an institutional profile, and separate chapters on academic programs, faculty, students, administration, budget and finances, and governance. An analysis, observations, and recommendations will be made regarding each of these areas.

THE VALUE OF AN INSTITUTIONAL REVIEW

The chair of the board of a major public university reported:

> We would never have found the president we did nor gotten him under way so effectively without an institutional review.

The chair of the board of a liberal arts college said:

> The review was a breath of new life and honesty for our entire college community and it served as the format from which we interviewed and evaluated our presidential candidates.

At the end of his first year in office, a university president declared:

> The review was the wisest thing I did. It gave me an expert, objective assessment of our condition and it served as the basis for my presidential strategy.

Another college president said:

> It would have taken me years to find out what we learned from the review in three months. Even though it was candid, it was celebrated by our entire community.

A sitting president reported:

> It's the only way we could overcome our own opinions, which had become encrusted by special interests, personal obligations, and preconceived opinions.

A review prepared in anticipation of the search process offers these benefits:

1. It is valuable to prospective candidates.
2. It enables the search committee to establish more than messianic criteria.

3. It helps the board address conditions during and before the appointment of a new president that would make the position more attractive to first-rank candidates. (For instance, a number of boards make changes in governance policies and practices between presidencies.)

4. The board and others become better and more accurately informed about the institution and develop more realistic expectations and plans.

5. In the case of public reviews, faculty, administrators, students, alumni, elected officials, benefactors, trustees, townspeople, and all other concerned parties are encouraged—indeed, bound—to consider a legitimate opinion of the institution that may differ from their own.

6. The region, state, and the entire universe of the institution gain a heightened awareness of and interest in the college or university because of their involvement in the review and their reading of the results. (At one major university, the local newspaper published the entire hundred-page review, and every newspaper in the state did feature stories and editorials.)

For a newly appointed president, in addition to the above, a review can:

1. ensure a better informed and more enlightened board by bringing to the board's attention important issues and potential problems affecting the institution;

2. help establish a tentative agenda for the institution and provide a more objective foundation for strategic and long-range planning;

3. serve as a dispassionate way to evaluate the organization and administration, the quality of academic programs, and the faculty and student body of an institution;

4. advise on the disposition of all constituencies including alumni, media, political bodies, and townspeople as well as faculty, staff, and students;

5. help determine the potential for increased private support;

6. provide a valuable substantive dimension to the inaugural year by informing the internal and external publics of the institution of the present condition of the institution and the forthright style of its new president;

7. prevent the new president's leadership potential from being diminished by not forcing him or her to make what might otherwise appear to be arbitrary judgments on important but controversial issues.

A sitting president finds an institutional review of value:

1. as an assessment of how things are going and what future plans (both institutional and personal) should include;

2. in preparing for accreditation and outside evaluation; a good review is far more valuable than the most thoughtful self-assessment;

3. as a check on other outside evaluations that may have been conducted from different or even opposing premises;

4. as a precursor to a presidential evaluation by the board.

The accomplishment of all these conditions does not risk the acceptance, credibility, or leadership of the president, because institutional problems and prospects are addressed by an outside authority who is not (or should not be) threatened by alienation, vested interests, or subtle reprisals from inside or outside the campus. Problems of funding, morale, personnel, organization, and governance can be addressed candidly without being colored by provincial interests and without diminishing the leadership potential of either the president or the board.

WHO CONDUCTS THE REVIEW?

The most important decision regarding an institutional review is deciding who should do it. The appointment criteria should include: (1) experience; (2) legitimacy; (3) chemistry; and (4) cost. Cost should be the least important criterion; whatever the cost, a good review is worth many times the price.

The person or firm you have in mind should have sufficient experience and provide you with copies of previous institutional reviews or assessments conducted, along with references. This is an important consideration. The quality of the review will be the primary determinant in the value of the effort. Don't be misled by the spoken word; ask to see evidence. The review team should include from three to six persons with impressive credentials; one person surely cannot do the job.

The person who chairs the team is of primary importance. He or she will organize the effort and finally write the report. This person must have experience in conducting such efforts. He or she should assemble the review team. Too often, the president, and sometimes the board, wants to name the people on the team, thereby raising questions about both validity and process. Feel free to suggest names, but don't press, for a good chair cannot be party even to the appearance of special interests.

How you feel about the person in charge of the review is obviously important. You should spend one-on-one time discussing the prospect, but it is even more significant that you consider the record of the individual (not the firm). If he or she has publications in the field, read them and make sure you are in general agreement with the author before proceeding further. Some authors write about the college presidency from the position of a strong presidency, while others take the "collegial" position. A team headed by a collegialist would undoubtedly have a somewhat different emphasis in many areas, particularly administration and governance. You make the choice, but never assume complete objectivity in another; the most you can expect is honesty, sophistication, and freedom from influence by your vested interest groups.

Again, cost should be the least important consideration in deciding on an institutional review. A good review is worth it, whatever the price. A complete review can run from $40,000 to $425,000, depending on the amount of time, the number of persons interviewed, and the reputation of the individual or firm conducting the review.

PREPARATION FOR THE REVIEW

Although the core of an institutional review is the visitation to the campus and surrounding area by the review team, the preparation for the review begins at least one month before the visit. After meeting with the commissioning authority (the board or the president), the chair of the review team takes charge of the process. He or she sends the following materials to each member of the team for reading in advance of the visit:

all catalogs, brochures, applications and promotional information;

all media coverage and press releases for the preceding twelve months;

budget and finance information (including procedures and recent audits);

past accreditation reports and any other outside evaluations;

an institutional membership list;

a profile of the student body (including five-year entering test scores and enrollment figures);

private support figures for the past five years and organizational and promotional materials;

the constitution and bylaws of the governing boards, the campus governance body, the alumni association and private foundations (if any) associated with the institution; along with names, titles, and home telephone numbers of all trustees and directors;

state-of-the-institution addresses and other papers of the incumbent president;

promotional materials on the surrounding community;

institutional and other planning documents; organizational chart(s); faculty, staff, and student handbooks; compensation figures for all employees;

institutional research reports; surveys conducted by or about the institution;

> information on the library, honors programs, placement records and graduate success of students;
>
> faculty publications; and any other information that may be of value to the team in conducting the review.

Finally, the chair of the team should ask key institutional officers to prepare confidential papers which will prove invaluable in preparing for the campus visit.

HOW A REVIEW IS CONDUCTED

After the appointment of a review team chair, he or she selects prospective team members on the basis of their particular strengths and on the special nature and needs of the institution. The team chair discusses the names and credentials of prospective team members with you, and, if acceptable, they are invited to serve on the team. Ordinarily, they are paid by the chair.

During a two-day or three-day visit to the campus(es), the review team conducts interviews, both individual and group, but all confidential. The interviews are the heart of the visitation and of the final report itself. The team interviews not only persons who have a special interest in the institution, but also outside authorities (persons in scholarly disciplines, national organizations, et al.). All interviews should follow a standardized format that allows an opportunity for interviewees to express any additional thoughts. Interviewees are selected because of position (trustees, faculty senate chair, senator, et al.) and at random. The team should select faculty by stratified random sample as well as at random and by position in campus governance.

No time should be scheduled for social amenities, but some ostensibly free time should be allowed for spontaneous interviews of people selected completely at random.

The team should receive the materials noted above at least two weeks prior to the visitation. They should also receive orientation materials from the team chair at an on-site meeting the evening before the interviews begin.

The team should work in a comfortable but neutral area (not the administration building) and should have on-site assistance. The ideal person would be an experienced staff administrator or secretary who schedules interviews and makes arrangements for the office space, transportation and lodging, and secretarial services.

Interviews are typically fifty minutes, and team members may interview by telephone those people who cannot conveniently come on-site. Frequently the team will do telephone interviews after the visit to assure that no important persons are left out of the review process. This is key, for everyone should be allowed to buy into this activity. If the team has the expertise, it can hold group sessions with separate groups (eight to fifteen) of faculty, students, alumni, and staff. These should follow the interview format.

At the conclusion of the visit, the team should have a brief private meeting, and then the chair of the team should meet with the commissioning authority.

After the visit, the team continues its evaluation of the institution, now including both written materials and the opinions of a hundred or so diverse parties. After six to nine weeks, the team submits a final written review. This is best done without additional comment. In-person presentations of such a document can lead to dialogue that obscures positions carefully considered and formulated after much thoughtful deliberation.

The value of an institutional review has never been questioned by boards, search committees, or presidents. The results have been embraced with great enthusiasm, for these are the building blocks of a stronger institution.

Chapter 6

Board and Campus Governance

The greatest deterrent to the re-establishment of the legitimate college presidency today is quite probably the state of board and campus governance. Both the condition of the college presidency and the research of effective leadership and organizational behavior speak strongly to this point.

I have reviewed the governance policies of over one hundred governing boards, and almost invariably they are laced with provisions that make an effective presidency difficult to impossible. After reviewing the bylaws of a prestigious but unhappy western liberal arts college, I advised the board (which, characteristically, was unaware of what it had done) that every time their president made a decision, she was putting her job on the line because she was in fact violating the constitutional authority of the faculty. The board changed its bylaws and everyone including the faculty was happier.

For more than three decades, I have watched as the office of the college or university president has been gradually, but measurably, diminished in stature and authority. While governing boards continue to hold college presidents accountable (as they should), the president has less and less authority to get the job done. The result has been lessened respect for the presidential office and for those who hold the position, and a growing tendency for governing boards to get overly involved in the administration of the institution. That involvement has led to ever closer relationships between boards and faculty, students and staff, thus increasing the estrangement of the president from each group. In such situations the leader, to survive at all, must become a master at pandering to each group until, almost inevitably, he or she succumbs to their collective ineptitude as the obvious scapegoat.

In such situations, effective leadership is all but impossible. Countless faculty petitions, board executive sessions, and harried presidents attest to this truth. The more fortunate presidents are eased out of office with golden handshakes, many fade into sad ignominy, some teeter into retirement, and some are simply fired for the wrong reasons. Too few weather the course with dignity.

Over the years, the governing boards of our institutions have granted faculty and students access and rights that were formerly privileges to be granted, denied, or withdrawn by college presidents. This condition, coupled with the faculty's historic notions of collegiality, gave rise to a neutered presidency. A presidency typically bereft of most of the established forms of effective leadership. Both of these conditions, over-involvement of faculty and students with governing boards and the fallacious notion of collegial leadership, have failed to meet the test when examined under the light of research and practice. Yet all too often, they continue to exist, unexamined by rational process.

The president's leadership potential is maximized only when the office is invested with sufficient status and authority to be taken seriously (the antithesis of collegiality). When this is the case, then the use of the incremental forms of leadership, expertise and charisma, is enhanced dramatically. It is only under these conditions that a president can effectively inspire trust and confidence in the college community. On the other hand, collegial relationships tend to evaporate during periods of stress or controversy. The hapless but still accountable leader becomes the scapegoat for his or her disjointed colleagues.

THE SOLUTION

The most direct way to restore the legitimate status of the presidential office is for a governing board to commission an outside review of all governance documents during the period of presidential transition. *Do not assume that you or anyone connected with the institution can do the job.* The institutional review discussed in Chapter 5 will include a governance review, but failing a full institutional review, a board must, at least, commission a governance review. Top-rank presidents have indicated that they would not have been attracted to their positions without such a review and the adoption of its results.

While this review of campus governance can take place under a sitting president, it should be commissioned by the board in deference to the sensitive role of the president, particularly vis-a-vis faculty. In this case, the board's job is to protect the president as this may be necessary, particularly when faculty members must be moved from intimate association in the board governance process.

Whether the institution has a newly appointed or a sitting president, only the governing board is able to rectify an eroded presidential office through a governance review. The advantage of doing it in a period of presidential transition is that it does not threaten a presidential incumbent, and at the same time it presents a more attractive position to presidential prospects.

Ordinarily, the person appointed as the general consultant for the presidential search is the logical choice to do the governance review. (Chapter 5 discusses this review in more detail.)

BASIC GOVERNANCE PREMISES

Although a university is a corporation, it differs from a business because of two conditions that are unique to education and that have come to be considered fundamental: academic freedom and shared governance. Two primary documents issued by the American Association of University Professors (AAUP) are accepted by most as standards against which the condition of a university is measured: the 1940 *Statement of Principles on Academic Freedom and Tenure* and the 1966 *Joint Statement on Government of Colleges and Universities* (Appendix M). Except in extreme cases, both faculty and administration consider these documents as essential roots for university governance.

Although some believe it is not possible to conduct an effective presidency under these premises, quite the contrary is true. The problem in many institutions has not been these concepts of academic freedom or shared governance. Rather, institutions often become stalled and enter conflict—in effect, leaderless because they become mired in their own faulty governance designs, ostensibly forged to protect or achieve these conditions. The unfortunate result has been that many boards and some faculty and administrators have come to question the concepts themselves. Yet neither concept is at all frightening or demanding; "The fault is not in our stars, but in ourselves. . . ."

THE 1940 STATEMENT OF PRINCIPLES ON ACADEMIC FREEDOM AND TENURE

The most important of the two is the 1940 *Statement of Principles on Academic Freedom and Tenure*. As a guiding standard, the *Statement* is a classic for American colleges and universities, and anyone who wants to breach it should give the matter the most thoughtful and enlightened consideration. Any decision in favor of abrogating it should be reconsidered.

The 1949 *Statement* was enacted after a series of joint conferences begun in 1934 between representatives of AAUP and the Association of American Colleges (AAC). Later, the *Statement* was officially endorsed by more than one hundred professional organizations. Briefly, academic freedom means freedom in teaching and research and is considered a fundamental declaration for the protection of the scholar-teacher and the student. Tenure is a means of ensuring academic freedom and enough economic security to make the profession attractive to persons of ability. Both conditions carry obligations on the part of the teacher, but *under certain conditions, tenured individuals can be terminated.*

Under academic freedom, the teacher is entitled to full freedom in research and publication of results, subject to the adequate performance of other academic duties. However, research for monetary return should be based on an understanding with the authorities of the institution. While the teacher is entitled to freedom in the classroom, controversial matters that have no relation to his or her subject are not protected. An example of this would be politics in a physics class. Any limitations required by religious or other purposes of the institution should be clearly articulated at the time of the teaching appointment.

When a teacher speaks or writes as a private citizen, there should be no institutional sanctions. Nonetheless, the *Statement* does call for the teacher to be "accurate, restrained, respectful of the opinions of others, and making every effort not to be perceived as a spokesperson for the institution." This was modified in 1970 as follows: "The controlling principle is that a faculty member's expression of opinion as a citizen cannot constitute grounds for dismissal unless it clearly demonstrates the faculty member's unfitness for his position." The 1970 interpretation also clarified that academic freedom applied to all who teach or hold academic rank including teaching assistants and those on probation.

Academic tenure means that at the end of a probationary period (not to exceed seven years), faculty should have continuous employment, subject to termination for adequate cause, except in the case of retirement for age or because of extraordinary financial exigencies. It is also advisable to give at least one year's notice if a person is to be terminated or not granted tenure at the end of the probationary period.

A few words about the termination of tenured faculty: if possible, the case should be considered by a representative faculty committee, in conjunction with the academic administration, and then forwarded to the governing boards by the president, with his or her recommendation. In such cases of dispute, the accused faculty member should be informed in writing of the reasons for dismissal, and he or she should have the opportunity to be heard by those who are bringing charges. In addition, the faculty member should have the right to be accompanied by an advisor and should have a full stenographic record of the proceedings.

Faculty who are dismissed for reasons other than "moral turpitude" should receive their salaries for at least one year from the date of notification of dismissal, whether or not they continue duties at the institution. It should be noted that moral turpitude is not defined as behavior offensive to the moral sensibilities of a particular community, but rather behavior that would be condemned by the academic community generally. Under extreme cases, the *Statement* calls for external review by the AAUP and AAC.

AAUP CENSORSHIP

Censorship by the AAUP for institutional violations of academic freedom or tenure was to be avoided at almost any cost. During recent years, largely because of the involvement of AAUP in collective bargaining, its decisions have been questioned, and AAUP censorship has come to mean less to most concerned parties, including not only board members but also many faculty and administrators. Many believe that recent changes in the emphasis of AAUP are not in keeping with the concept of shared governance (discussed later in this chapter). While governing boards and presidents should acknowledge the importance of the practice of academic freedom and the conditions of tenure, generally they need not be as concerned about the prospect of AAUP censorship.

THE 1966 JOINT STATEMENT ON GOVERNMENT OF COLLEGES AND UNIVERSITIES (APPENDIX N)

At the outset, it is important to note that although the *Statement* is promulgated as the "joint" statement of the American Association of University Professors, the American Council on Education (ACE), and the Association of Governing Boards of Universities and Colleges (AGB), ACE and AGB did not actually endorse it. Rather, both stated that they "recognized the *Statement* as a significant step forward in the clarification of the respective jobs of governing boards, faculties, and administrations and "condemned" it to institutions and governing boards. The *Statement*, in any case, is not intended to serve as a blueprint or as a defense in controversy among the various interested parties of an institution, nor does the *Statement* cover relations with state systems and other outside agencies.

While the Statement emphasizes the role of the faculty, in several places it clearly states that the faculty "recommends" to the president (or a presidential delegate), who then acts or in turn "recommends" to the governing board. It speaks to the "initiating capacity and decision-making *participation*" of all of the institutional parties and of differences in "weight" of each voice determined by the responsibility of each party for the particular matter under consideration. The *Statement* makes valid points about the generally debilitating nature of unilateral action and the importance of standard procedures for areas of responsibility, authority, and continuing review.

It states that: the faculty's primary area of responsibility should be to determine the curriculum "after an educational goal has been established." But even here, it points out that the final institutional *authority* is the president and the governing board. It should be emphasized that a president or a governing board rarely makes any academic judgment other than to ask the faculty to reconsider an academic matter.

The *Statement* also recommends that faculty and, to a lesser degree, students be involved in long-range planning, decisions regarding existing or prospective physical resources, budgeting, the appointment of the president, and the appointment of chief academic officers. Note that the *Statement* says nothing about the evaluation of the president or other institutional officers. The idea that faculty might be involved in this area is of fairly recent vintage and, like many other board and campus practices today, without compelling foundation in either history or logic.

The *Statement* does not call for direct formal contact between the faculty and the governing board, but rather for faculty (and student) to forward recommendations to the president who may or may not endorse their positions to the board. It calls for the president to convey "faculty views, including dissenting views" to the board and asks the president to inform the faculty of the board's position. Although it asks for communication, it does *not* ask for faculty (or student) membership on board committees or on the board itself.

Unfortunately, many governing boards as well as some presidents (and many faculty politicians) have misunderstood this call for faculty participation in decision-making as a demand for close association between all of the decision-making parties. This has understandably resulted in countless instances of board/faculty/student formal associations, each with the potential of compromising the role and the ability of one another and, most unfortunately, of the president. The faculty member or student will say, "If I can get it from the board, why bother with the president?" The accountable, and hopefully agile, president is left dancing between the two. All three parties are less happy and less effective. When things go bad, and they invariably do, the president and other administrators pay the bill.

In sum, the governance problems in our colleges and universities do not arise from the unique concepts of academic freedom and shared governance. Rather, the fault lies in the implementation of these concepts. Neither statement suggests intimate association of the participating parties. Yet, scholars write, presidents (perhaps wisely) accede, and national associations advocate the very things that could be the undoing of our uniqueness, and governing boards continue to put presidents between a rock and a hard place. Under such circumstances, presidents cannot lead, boards cannot govern, faculties are politicized, and no one can be held accountable.

Chapter 7

Presidential Evaluation (Review)

A successful presidential evaluation should accomplish two things: (1) fulfill the board's responsibility to evaluate the president, and (2) increase the legitimacy of the presidential office. It is in this last area that most evaluations fall woefully short. Increasingly boards employ evaluation techniques that compromise the ability of the president to lead. This chapter describes a method that can objectively determine the performance of the president and at the same time enhance the importance of the presidential office, that is, make it more possible for the president to lead and be held accountable.

This most sensitive and delicate responsibility of the governing board, the evaluation of the president, should be approached more thoughtfully than any methods currently offered in the higher education literature or by mainstream organizations. Although accountability is basic to the idea of granting more legitimacy to the presidential office, the need for accountability should be satisfied by the governing board in a way that does not diminish the presidential office in the process. (I call this procedure a "presidential review" because, as with an institutional review, other terms tend to have pejorative connotations.)

Equal in importance to the appointment and support of the president, is the presidential evaluation as it is an even more complex responsibility of the board, for poorly conducted presidential reviews can and have compromised otherwise effective presidencies.

Most presidential evaluations *are* poorly conducted. Far too often a board of trustees, while conscientiously trying to satisfy its important review obligation, effectively reduces the authority and potential of its chief executive officer. Indeed, distinguished presidents have resigned from office on the heels of ostensibly "objective" presidential evaluations, and others have left in even less comfortable circumstances.

THE HISTORY OF PRESIDENTIAL EVALUATIONS

Formal or systematic presidential review first gained credence in 1969 when a besieged Kingman Brewster, then president of Yale University, endorsed the idea in an article entitled "The Politics of the Academy," published in *School and Society*. During that period, an unprecedented number of governing boards and presidents were making concessions to the pressing wave of democratization described in Chapter 1. Faculty and students began to appear on governing boards, usually with presidential endorsement, or at least acquiescence. Soon faculty, students, and staff came to expect as rights conditions that presidents formerly had granted as privileges. In many instances, what governing boards didn't give away, faculty and staff organizations, and often unions, were able to gain by threat and intimidation.

Institutions had achieved the epitome of collegial leadership, a completely accountable president with no real authority. In many institutions, the president became no more than a symbol in higher education's "shared governance." There was little left about which a president could be benevolent. According to national panels, commissions, and scholars, presidential leadership in colleges and universities was at an all time low.

The same period of dramatic decline in leadership gave birth to informal and formal presidential evaluation or assessment, a practice now followed by more than 85 percent of colleges and universities. Today, many believe presidential evaluation, particularly "formal" presidential evaluation as currently presented by mainstream publications and national organizations and practiced by most governing boards, has been the most significant factor in the decline of the American college presidency.

The practice of presidential evaluation is relatively new, and, for a procedure so critical to the conduct of an institution, there is a dearth of literature and virtually no significant substantive research. Since Brewster's article in 1969, scarcely more than a dozen people have written on the subject and only a handful with any regularity. There is only one "authoritative guide" on the subject: John W. Nason's *Presidential Assessment* (1984), a publication of the Washington, DC-based Association of Governing Boards of Universities and Colleges (AGB).

CONVENTIONAL WISDOM ON PRESIDENTIAL REVIEW

Nason writes of two methods for presidential assessment: informal and formal.

Informal evaluations tend to be more frequent. . . "at least once a year" . . .They are conducted by the board as a whole or by the executive committee—occasionally there may be an individual board member or special committee appointed for the specific purpose. The trustees may or may not make inquiries of faculty, administrative officers, students, alumni, and others, but such inquiries are likely to be casual and unsystematic. Their information may come largely from rumors floating about the campus. . . .They have a confidential character. . .and are certainly not heralded nor their results publicized (Nason, 1984).

On the other hand:

Formal evaluations are regularly scheduled every three, four, or five years. They involve an organized and systematic effort to get objective evidence. . . .Sometimes questionnaires are distributed widely to faculty, students, alumni, and others. . .and they are public (Nason, 1984).

Nason wisely states that the evidence suggests that formal evaluations are likely to generate as many negative consequences as positive ones, and, although he doesn't say so, you could conclude that he feels the same way about the informal method. He then provides a glimpse of an "Ideal Design" based on his survey of college and university governing boards (Nason, 1984). But the reader is left wondering about this attractive prospect, for Nason devotes most of the remainder of the book to describing how to conduct these same questionable methods of "evaluation." While he advises caution, he concludes that formal evaluations seem to be the order of the day and offers everything from procedural advice to sample letters, questionnaires, rating scales, and evaluation instruments.

Regardless of the outcome of such a process, all of these techniques lead to a significantly reduced presidency. They are an absolute contradiction of what we know about the conditions that ensure effective leadership.

THE PROBLEM WITH CONVENTIONAL WISDOM

Most formal and many informal evaluations achieve the exact opposite of their intended effect. While the presidents who receive poor evaluations are usually eased out of office, those who continue (the great majority) do so with less stature and less authority. Faculty members and even staff and students are led to believe, at least implicitly, that they have a "vote" in the president's tenure. Board members (and often presidential evaluators) frequently establish undermining contacts with faculty, staff, and students. Indeed, the condition became so bad that the State University of New York replaced formal assessment with informal periodic review. My contention is that SUNY, like many others, was simply doing formal evaluations the wrong way. *Indeed, in order to do its job properly, the governing board should commission periodic formal evaluations. At least every five years.*

Periodic formal review is by far the most effective way that a board can accomplish this basic responsibility of evaluating the president. The question then is how to do it, not whether or not it should be done.

The major problem with most methods of presidential review is that they *publicly* involve members of the president's primary leadership constituency (faculty, students, and staff) in the review process. By involving these people they diminish, albeit unintentionally, the status of the presidential office and the leadership ability and potential of the president.

Why are most presidential assessments diminishing, polarizing, and, in the long run, demoralizing to the entire community? When faculty members, students, and staff are given reason by a board to believe they control the leader, the resulting attitude compromises both the presidential position and the president's potential for leadership.

Leadership is not rooted in collegiality. As Max Weber concluded years ago: "Collegiality is not democratic; rather, it is as elitist as a monarchy. It is simply that a select group of people share in the power. Indeed, if the collegials can wrest all the power away from the leader, they will prove every bit as self-serving as the most dissolute monarch" (Weber, 1947). The problem is that a board can't hold a group of collegials accountable, but it can replace a president. Unaccountable conditions give rise to irresponsible representations that force collegiality to break down under conditions of tension and conflict.

Leadership is rooted in the leader's ability to empower others by inspiring trust and confidence. In order to achieve trust and confidence, not only must the leader be professionally qualified but, even more important, the position he or she holds must be invested with sufficient legitimacy (authority) for the president to be able to lead. A president so invested is sufficiently ensconced so that he or she can be both engaging and giving in conducting the presidential office. The president can grant privileges to members of the community, faculty, staff, and students. The president can be benevolent because the president is, in fact, *the president.*

There are those who assume that if the members of the college or university community know the board is conducting a presidential review, they must be involved and, in effect, have a vote. Otherwise, the faculty will insist on some type of involvement or set in motion its own evaluation.

If a board believes that it has an objective method of evaluating the president, it should not respond affirmatively to self-motivated faculty evaluations. Beyond academic freedom, which should be rooted in a board tenure policy, what other unique conditions does the institution owe a faculty member: in the strictest terms, *nothing.*

While shared governance is a desirable and potentially effective condition, at most institutions it was originally a privilege that presidents granted to faculty members and, to a lesser extent, students. They were encouraged to participate in the decision-making process, subject to the final authority of the president.

This system worked rather well. Faculty and students became importantly involved in decision-making, and a dialogue was established that almost invariably led to a better institution. But through time and societal circumstances, the role of the president in this decision-making process became more and more a token one. The time came when it was woe to most presidents to question the prerogatives of the faculty. Academic freedom had been extended beyond the individual to include the collective faculty, and today few presidents can afford to take serious issue with the faculty.

Many governing boards and even respected national associations appear to assume the faculty is autonomous in academic affairs and entitled to have an authoritative hand in all matters affecting the institution. Under such circumstances, presidential accountability is impossible. As we established in Chapter 6, the faculty is not, in fact, autonomous, for there is no hallmark document that calls for absolute faculty authority even in academic matters.

Proof of the unbalanced condition is the idea that, if you do not involve faculty in presidential review, they will demand to be involved and it will be done. Governing boards must stand above any debate. If need be, they must declare that there is only one chief executive and he or she is accountable for the conduct of all affairs of the institution. (If this means changing board policies, and it usually does, it should be done.)

Should the accountable president choose to delegate responsibility and authority (and the wise one will), then so be it. That decision must be the president's. Only under these conditions can the president remain the truly accountable officer and be evaluated in that light. This also means that there are no formal relationships between the board and faculty, staff, and students, except those that are recommended by the ultimately accountable officer, the president. Under these conditions, as discussed in the preceding chapter, shared governance can work beautifully; affected people are involved in decision-making, yet the president is clearly the final and accountable authority.

HOW TO CONDUCT AN EFFECTIVE PRESIDENTIAL EVALUATION

A board that is conducting an annual informal presidential evaluation should consider the following procedure:

1. The president drafts a Modified Institutional Management by Objectives (MIMBO) for presentation to the governing board in the spring of the academic year preceding the evaluation. The MIMBO is the most important dimension of an informal presidential evaluation. The president may do the initial draft in consultation with close associates, but in the final analysis, the draft is the president's. The document should include both specific and general goals; the specific goals are more readily measurable, and the general goals allow and, indeed, inspire the president to conduct the presidential office in pursuit of the grander vision of the institution. Concentrating exclusively on specific goals would force the president to adopt management tendencies and would reduce his or her leadership potential.

2. The president presents the MIMBO to the board chair. The chair and the president then have a thoughtful private discussion during which the MIMBO may be modified, subject to the acceptance of both. At this point, the MIMBO can be presented to the full board as a document endorsed, at least tacitly, by the board chair, representing the goals of the president for the coming year.

3. At the end of the academic year, the president prepares a written statement responding to the MIMBO. The statement is discussed with the board chair and then presented to the full board, preferably in executive session. An executive session (without the public or staff, faculty, or students) fosters a dialogue that can prove helpful to both the board and the president without threatening the importance of the presidential office. If an executive session with the full board is not possible, the president should make the MIMBO presentation to the executive committee of the board.

4. The board meets in executive session, absent the president.

5. The president then meets with the board or the executive committee of the board for a more specific discussion of the MIMBO and the coming year.

6. Interviews should not be conducted in conjunction with annual evaluations, nor should board members have "informal" chats with staff or faculty.

7. Outside consultants are generally not used in conducting informal presidential evaluations.

THE FORMAL PRESIDENTIAL EVALUATION

The board should commission a formal presidential evaluation about every five years. Whatever the method used, it should not include the public involvement of faculty, students, and staff. *This condition is crucial to the preservation of the legitimate presidency.*

The board should conduct the evaluation in confidence and with the endorsement of the president. If the evaluator interviews faculty, staff, or students, he or she should represent the interviews as a review of the condition of the institution, rather than as an evaluation of the president. (In reality a formal presidential evaluation *is* a mini-evaluation of the institution.)

A board that plans a formal presidential evaluation should consider the following:

1. Use of outside third-party consultation. If a thorough and fair evaluation is to be done, it *must* be done by a tested outside consultant. The board chair should engage the consultant with the approval of the president.

2. Review of the annual Modified Institutional Management by Objectives (MIMBO), discussed above. If MIMBOs have not been used in the past, start the process here. Ask your consultant for advice about design and procedure.

3. The president should prepare a confidential self-review for the consultant following guidelines provided by the consultant. Among other things, it should include the president's response to whatever goals have been pursued during the time frame of the evaluation.

4. Several weeks prior to the campus visitation, the consultant should receive a package of pertinent materials including: a general catalogue; other catalogs, if any; fiscal reports, including the most recent outside audit; institutional promotional pieces; private support record and admissions profile for the preceding five years; media coverage for the six-month period preceding the review; presidential speeches; faculty preparation conditions and publications; line staff charts; board and campus governance bylaws, policies, and minutes; institutional self-studies; and any other materials relating to the substance or disposition of the institution.

5. Interviews with trustees and members of the non-primary leadership constituency (e.g., all board members, alumni, newspaper editors and publishers, elected officials, appointed officials, benefactors, business persons, leaders of minority groups, et al.).

6. After arriving on campus, the consultant should select faculty, students, and staff to interview. Any other approach seriously compromises the legitimacy of the presidential office and reduces the potential of the incumbent. The consultant should select the interviewees by position (e.g., chair of faculty senate), stratified random sample, and at random.

7. The consultant should write an evaluation report and present it to the chair of the board, with a copy for the president. Preferably, the consultant presents the president's copy in an off-campus setting. The evaluation should include sections on: (a) overview, (b) academic programming, (c) faculty, (d) students, (e) administration, (f) budget and finance, (g) private support; alumni, public, and government relations, (h) governance, (i) presidential style, and (j) observations and recommendations. The full report *should not* be made public because of the unnecessary and potentially harmful dimensions of public exposure.

If the board handles the process sensitively, it will gain a valuable assessment of the institution, its people, policies, practices, and its president. The incumbent will be closely and objectively evaluated, and the presidential office will be enhanced rather than diminished.

Chapter 8

A Helpful Entrance To A Long Tenure and A Graceful Exit: Presidential Compensation

The genesis of this chapter came from a two-day seminar with the presidents of the public and private colleges and universities of a large midwestern state. After establishing a healthy rapport with a lively discussion of the presidency and effective relationships with the board, the faculty, the students, staff, and the various external constituencies, one president of a selective private institution asked in exasperation, "But how the hell does one get out of this office gracefully?" Immediately, his spirit was joined by those of his fellow presidents, and we spent the remainder of the afternoon in stimulating, but essentially nonproductive discussion. We also talked at length about the generally unhappy state of the presidency and how difficult it was to attract top people to the position (present company excepted, of course). As I left, I promised to study the prospect and to try to develop a reasonably inclusive set of ideas and strategies for governing boards and presidents to consider.

I subsequently discussed the subject with several groups of trustees. While their concern was as serious, their emphasis was somewhat different. They wanted to know of graceful ways to ease out presidents who were losing their touch. They were equally concerned about keeping presidents whose reputations were so outstanding that they were frequently sought out by other institutions. "How do you hold on to a really good president without reacting in the heat of an alternative offer?" was a frequently asked question. Too often boards report that they have lost first-rate presidents because they had not anticipated the possibility of a better, alternative offer.

THE PRESIDENT WHO SHOULD LEAVE

Virtually all presidents know when their time is up. The problem is that they usually have no comfortable or satisfactory alternative. The declining president continues in office, and the institution, and its people, pay the price for want of a graceful way out. To compensate for inattention or ineffectiveness, the president usually appoints additional staff, making the institution administratively top-heavy and even more costly and ineffective. The appointment of an executive vice president, or some other title, ostensibly to manage the internal affairs of the institution is sometimes a sign that this is happening. The life and vigor of the institution diminish. Others of lesser station and perspective fill the leadership vacuum ineffectively. The institution and its people suffer.

The leadership of the governing board knows this truth, but things are not really bad enough to make a case for dismissing the president. Besides, he or she has only a few years to retirement. The situation continues in a frustrating, endless maze as the board treats the symptoms rather than the real problem—the president. The great wrong is that both the board and the president know there is no fail-safe mechanism for the president to gently and gracefully engage to leave the office. Both have neglected to do anything about it, and now it is too late.

Case One:

A well-meaning board was convinced that its nine-year president, who was four years away from retirement, was hurting the institution. With the knowledge and support of the president, the board appointed an executive vice president. The president did not know that the board had asked this new executive vice president to really run the university and to report in confidence to the executive committee of the board. Within months, virtually everyone knew what was happening. The board was confronted with an incredulous president, unhappy alumni and benefactors, and a divided faculty. The president retired, the executive vice president resigned. At last report, the board had been forced to extend its presidential search for want of good candidates.

Case Two:

In another situation, the burned-out president of seventeen years asked to be relieved of his presidential duties and be appointed chancellor, primarily for external and fund-raising purposes. This was done and now, eight years later, the institution has had three presidents whose every move has been overshadowed by the omnipresent chancellor. The faculty has been demoralized, private support has gone down, yet the chancellor continues on.

Case Three:

A fourteen-year president, in a small private college, was wavering. A compassionate board thought it could carry him to retirement by assuming an increasingly larger portion of the presidential burden.

The executive committee would meet more often, and the board chair, a strong woman, would move into a more prominent position in center stage. Three years later, the staff and faculty, initially happy to have such close contact with the board, were demoralized. Both the enrollment and the endowment had gone down. The president, ostensibly the one to be served by the arrangement, retired—dispirited and undignified.

Case Four:

A seven-year president of a medium-sized public university knew he was running out of gas. When he became president, morale was at an all-time low, the academic program was in disarray, accreditation was in trouble, and the reputation of the institution was definitely second-rate. His first years had been dynamic and productive. Spirits soared, and everyone was filled with the excitement of his enthusiastic leadership. The president appeared tireless. It seemed he spoke some place every night and always made an appearance at the important social and civic functions. Yet he was also highly visible on the campus to faculty, staff, and students.

His workdays were usually fifteen hours or longer. During one three-month period he was not able to have dinner at home with his family even once.

The curriculum had been tightened, a greater number of better students were enrolling, faculty and staff were energized anew, and private support had developed significantly. The region and the state took special pride in their university. The university was often noted for excellence and listed as outstanding among institutions of its type.

This continued into the seventh year. The president was beginning to tire. He wanted out. Not interested in another presidency, he continued in office as problems went unattended and his enthusiasm continued to wane.

The university gradually returned to its former sleepy, unhappy state. Ten years later the unhappy president was still in office.

Case Five:

A distinguished state system president of long term was forced to resign in a power play by a politically ambitious new board chair. The now former president, out of a job, did all she could to undermine efforts by the board to appoint an able successor. Finally, the board appointed a "home-grown" business type to the position. Ten years later the state still suffers from the damage done.

For confirmation and perspective on the subject, I asked a distinguished, long-tenured president to comment on my observations. He wrote the following response.

I have read and reread Chapter 8 a number of times. On Sunday afternoon, it was raining and I started again, this time from a different perspective. I outlined the thirteen presidential changes, entries, and/or exits I have observed closely and looked at them as dispassionately as possible in terms of your proposals and examples.

I would have to say that the majority fit, in one way or another, the substance of your contention. Most smart of a brutality that was uncalled for under any circumstance, created long-standing scars within the constituencies and demeaned the board as well as the president. Two, on the other hand, did not. Both were marked by two notable situations. In one, the outgoing president was given leave for one year as the new president took office and, in fact, returned to the campus as a "distinguished professor" carrying, strangely enough, all of the perquisites you describe. The other was a retirement that followed another part of your scenario wherein the individual, in fact, was provided a very healthy annuity plan to allow retirement without a significant change in economic status.

The other eleven were clouded by poorly conceived, if not trumped-up, reasons for the president stepping aside stated by various members of the board. In short, I can't find a flaw in your observation or definition of the problem.

Realistically, an effective president, age fifty-five-plus, doesn't have many options unless they are created years in advance. Few are intellectually dead, and the professorship/retirement planning option seems to be a "best of all worlds" proposal for the institution and the president.

I think there is another scenario that is unspoken which can or could be created should the professorship route not be a viable long-term one. Your Case Four president in fact ought to step out after seven years. After age 55, one seeks not to look at another "top spot." With ten to twenty productive years still available, what the institution does in handling his step-down has a marked influence on his return to the academy in a new role, even at another institution. In this case, the board has special responsibilities for the well-being of the president professionally. All too often the board doesn't choose to face them and lets it appear as a "forced step-down." The institution suffers because of a real split in the institutional constituencies, and the ex-president suffers the consequences in the relocation process.

Your scenarios and solutions are completely applicable to the "older folk" among us who have served well and now should be cut loose for the good of the institution. I wonder how many young talents we drive away by not making the transition out a good one in the eyes of our colleagues.

THE EFFECTIVE PRESIDENT WHO MIGHT HAVE STAYED

Governing boards are too often confronted with able presidents who opt to move to other institutions for reasons that appear to be nebulous. Although rarely discussed, almost invariably compensation is one of the roots, if not the most important root, of presidential departure. How many presidents do you know who have gone elsewhere for less money? Yet approximately 500 presidencies turn over each year, and more than half of those go on to other presidencies. In 1986, according to our study, most of those who moved were among the most effective presidents in the nation.

Case One:

The president of a public institution, which had achieved a veritable rebirth under his leadership, has become a topic on the national scene. Invited to write articles, present papers, and provide informal consulting on the source of his success, the president is frequently contacted by search committees and head-hunters who try to tempt him with ever more attractive offers. Now in his fourth year, the president knows that his reputation will not suffer if he leaves, and he begins to occasionally accept invitations to consider other presidencies. One looms as particularly attractive. It offers a compensation package that is considerably better than his present situation. The president goes to his board chair, an experienced businesswoman, who knows that one should not compete with an uncertain outside bid and, instead, tells the president that she will do her very best the next time his contract is considered. The president leaves and is replaced by what the board considers a pale facsimile.

Case Two:

A five year president in a small, liberal arts college has received a most appealing offer from another institution. During his tenure, enrollment has increased, academic standards have gone up, and costs have gone down. The endowment of the college has increased from $12 to $35 million and is still climbing. When initially appointed, the president was of limited experience, and the board felt in no position to offer more than a minimum compensation package. Through the ensuing successful years, a few conservative board members who felt that the president's "call to serve" was sufficient to ensure his staying were able to lull other board members into doing little to increase presidential compensation. The president, a man with three children in school, felt "called" to go elsewhere for double his salary along with other compensations. After years in neutral, the board appointed a new president at essentially the same compensation level its former president earned at his new college. The impact of the new president is still an unknown to the board.

Case Three:

The highly effective president of a land-grant university leaves to accept the presidency of a small liberal arts college, declaring that he feels drawn to the serene, contemplative life of a small college in a small town, where a college president is still involved in the collegial life. It is also true that the small liberal arts college pays almost one-third more in salary than the land-grant university and has, along with a more generous retirement program, offered life insurance, disability insurance, and a special annuity plan. The president departs, in spite of the fact that the land-grant university has a private foundation that could have legally provided an attractive compensation package.

Case Four:

The board of a small private college is perplexed. It has gone through five presidents in fourteen years, and four of them have left of their own volition, enjoying the full support of the board. Each has gone on to accept a presidency elsewhere. "It couldn't be the president's compensation package," stated the board chair. "We match all our figures with the national compensation studies."

Case Five:

The universally admired president of a land-grant university leaves to accept the presidency of a regional public university in a neighboring state.

In four years the president has turned around the land-grant university; she has reduced costs, streamlined the curriculum, increased the percentage of state funds allocated to the university, and raised the morale of faculty and citizens. The regional public university quite literally used its foundation to buy away the land-grant president and then insured itself through an attractive pair of golden handcuffs.

Virtually all of these cases, as well as countless other variations on the same themes could have been avoided if the board had considered the prospect of presidential departure before the appointment was made, or before the presidential nadir or job-change process began.

OTHER CONSIDERATIONS A BOARD SHOULD MAKE IN APPOINTING A PRESIDENT

The Former President(s)

The clean and timely separation of the former president should be accomplished before the new president begins. This separation is the job of the board. There are countless examples of boards that have neglected this sensitive relationship. In one situation, a former president continued to receive mail in the president's office for ten years and came around personally to pick it up! In another, the former president continued to live on the campus and to be visible and obvious at campus events. In a third, the former president became a member of the board; indeed, in at least one situation, there were five former presidents on the board!

Former presidents should get out of the way, literally as well as figuratively. Ideally, they should leave the community, at least for a year, preferably at institutional expense. This year-long hiatus should also apply to the former president who assumes a professorship upon leaving office. It is the job of the board to ensure that this transition is accomplished smoothly.

COMPENSATION PACKAGES

In recent years, boards have implemented a number of innovations to avoid these unfortunate conditions. Increasingly, more governing boards in both sectors are providing extraordinary compensation packages for effective incumbent presidents. They are doing this as a lure for outstanding presidential prospects and as a way to retain them, as well as a safety valve should problems develop along the way. In such cases, both the board and the president have a relatively easy way out, a way that need not be plagued with confrontation or acrimony.

Compensation packages include the traditional items of salary, housing, automobiles, domestic help, an entertainment allowance, and a conventional retirement plan. These packages often include salary supplements, tenured professorships, sabbatical leave provisions, higher contributions to retirement, special annuities, life and disability insurance, multi-year contracts, and other attractive conditions. Many also include less formal provisions for outside income such as corporate board membership, consulting arrangements, and speaking honoraria.

PROCEDURES

The board that wishes to develop an attractive compensation package to retain an incumbent president should begin by appointing, with the concurrence of the president, an outside executive compensation firm of impressive reputation (the importance of appointing a firm of stature cannot be overstated). If the package is being developed to offer to a new president, the board should retain the firm at the start of the search, and the recommended package should be tailored to the special interests of the final candidate. Although top presidential prospects rarely speak at length about compensation, they are mightily impressed by a board that makes such special efforts in this sensitive but very important area.

The consultant should make final recommendations to the board in executive session. The recommendations should be based on a sophisticated analysis of comparative compensation conditions and the particular needs of the president.

Boards should not be overly impressed with the results of national presidential compensation studies, regardless of the source. Average figures in such studies, as well as the range of compensation, are invariably low because unusual prerequisites are not always reported, and boards with impressive compensation packages for their presidents *rarely participate in national studies.* Internal Revenue Service records can be checked, but these usually carry information about current income only and do not include deferred-income plans, which the astute president may find even more appealing than current earnings.

THE GOLDEN HANDCUFFS

Increasingly, governing boards are considering additional ways to retain effective presidents. In the past they have relied on salary and other compensatory items, competitive retirement systems, and even more uncertain conditions such as a uniquely attractive local environment and institutional appeal. Boards have either assumed that these forms of specific and poetic honoraria will be sufficient to hold the president or they have simply failed to come to grips with the uncomfortable prospect of losing a president until it is too late.

An attractive compensation package might cover all of these items, among others: board memberships, consulting fees and honoraria, insurance programs, unusual retirement packages, multi-year contracts, special annuities and trusts, and special spousal considerations. Often many or all of these are considered by governing boards as ways to keep an outstanding president (Appendixes O, P, and Q).

Particularly noteworthy is the so-called "rabbi trust," initially used to keep winning football and basketball coaches on board. (Appendix Q) (Another example of the deplorable imbalance in higher education: these pioneering efforts came first for the athletic coach.) In effect, a rabbi trust guarantees the beneficiary a pot of gold at the end of a prearranged period, usually five to ten years. The trust assumes certain conditions (i.e., the recipient continues to be a winner). This means that the president continues to fulfill the expectations of the governing board and to meet or exceed all of the evaluation criteria.

The board's expectations are spelled out in at least two contracts, a standard employment contract containing such stipulations as the period of employment, duties, salary, additional entitlements (hospitalization, disability insurance, retirement provisions, vacation, sick leave, residence and expenses, sabbatical leave, entertainment reimbursement, automobile, and other special considerations such as professional employment conditions for the spouse), termination and presidential evaluation or review.

Additional contractual relationships contain a provision by which the board retains the right to discharge the president. The terms of a rabbi trust are not fulfilled until the president has completed a prescribed period of effective service as determined by the board. For tax purposes, this trust is designed so that there is "no significant evidence of ownership" on the part of the recipient.

Funding such trusts is also important, particularly within public institutions. Funding is usually under the aegis of a private foundation operating in conjunction with the institution and is sometimes made contingent upon an increased level of private support. This avoids using otherwise designated funds for this purpose. (Appendix R)

The role of the president's spouse has changed dramatically during recent years. For instance, in one state only one of ten presidents of public institutions was married to his or her original spouse, and five of them had remarried during their presidential tenure. Increasingly, boards need to recognize that they should consider professional *couples* and show interest in helping the spouse find suitable employment. The traditional spouse is changing, and, in the interest of both presidential employment and retention, boards must recognize this development.

Women presidents face special problems. If they are married, what outside employment and role expectations should be anticipated for the spouse? Spousal stipends should also be considered. If they are not married, there are also problems. In one state, a single woman president asked the board for a $35,000-plus person who would do for her what many "traditional" wives do without compensation. At this writing, the issue was still unresolved. The board was seeking a way to keep this capable woman president happy, yet it faced the possibility of having to provide stipends to the spouses of all future presidents.

If the board is willing to address these problems thoughtfully, a president will consider leaving a good situation more carefully, and many will not consider it at all.

THE GOLDEN PARACHUTE

Perhaps the most widely used practice in both the public and the private sector is for boards to allow presidents who have served for five or more years to opt for special professorships. An impressive number of institutions are granting a tenured faculty position at the time of the presidential appointment. The position usually carries these provisions:

1. tenure;
2. at least 80 percent of the top salary earned by the president while in office;
3. a full year sabbatical to be used for transition and retooling;
4. a teaching load, if any, of no more than six to nine hours;
5. comfortable office space and clerical assistance;
6. reporting directly to the chief academic officer of the institution to ensure that any teaching or other service for an academic department would be considered a bonus by the department; and
7. a president emeritus title.

In state systems, the departing president is sometimes assigned to other campuses or to the system office. The quid pro quo is that the former president must not be involved in institution-wide efforts or in other ways "get in the hair" of his or her successor.

The key here is that the sitting president can, in effect, gracefully and without controversy, choose to move to a professorship for this option is "writ in stone" in board policy long before the fact. Had these policies been in effect earlier, they would have saved the dynamics of countless institutions, as well as the dignity of their presidents. Indeed, to get an ineffective president out of office in such a comparatively effortless manner would be cheap at many times the cost. Yet most boards continue to be sustained by the thought that the president can go on forever with the hope that serious problems will not develop.

IN SUM

The reader should bear in mind that all of these features serve to the mutual advantage of both the president and the board. A thoughtful presidential compensation package is a significant factor in every presidential decision, from attracting the right candidate, to keeping a sitting president happy, to having a graceful pre-established form for presidential departure. The astute governing board considers both the presidential compensation package and a special professorship for its president. Such a board is better able to serve its institution for it provides its president with "golden handcuffs," and a "golden parachute." For the effective president, it is hard to leave. For the president past his or her prime, there is a graceful way out.

Chapter 9

Responsibilities of a Governing Board

This book has dealt primarily with the five most fundamental responsibilities of a governing board—presidential appointment, presidential review or evaluation, presidential support (notably compensation), board policies and institutional governance, and institutional evaluation. We should also consider other important responsibilities that can contribute to the restoration or establishment of a more accountable college presidency.

It is the responsibility of the board chair and the president to assure the proper orientation of trustees. Indeed, the education of board members is essential to their constructive participation. Many assume that otherwise sophisticated board members need no further education regarding the governance of a college or university. Typically, the most sophisticated board members are most in need of special orientation in enlightened higher education governance. If not, things may go smoothly. . .until there are problems, and then it is too late.

I was once invited by the board chair and the president to do an orientation session for the board of a midwestern public university because of *one* trustee who persisted in meddling in administration. I went to the session primed for rational conversion. The trustee didn't show up. As it turned out, he was advising the vice president for academic affairs about how to organize the academic services of the university. The moral of the story: schedule orientation sessions *before* problems develop.

The offerings of the Association of Governing Boards of Universities and Colleges are so respected that AGB's list of governing board responsibilities has come to be almost generic for colleges and universities. This list, with noted modifications, serves as a point of departure in the following presentation. The reader should bear in mind that these responsibilities are critiqued in appreciation for the good work of AGB and John Nason, the AGB's principal author.

91

As with corporate boards, boards in higher education are both the highest authority and the body ultimately accountable for the conduct of the institution. The following are generally accepted as the responsibilities of a governing board:

1. to appoint the president;
*2. to evaluate the institution;
*3. to assess board policies;
4. to support the president;
5. to review the performance of the president;
6. to renew the mission;
7. to approve the long–range plans;
8. to oversee the programs;
9. to ensure financial solvency;
10. to preserve organizational independence;
*11. to represent both the institution and the public;
12. to serve as a court of appeal;
13. to determine board performance.

All of these responsibilities are discussed here in view of a more legitimate presidency. Additions (points 2, 3, and 11) and modifications are designed to facilitate significant participation of all concerned parties within the provisions of the AAUP *Statement of Principles on Academic Freedom and Tenure* and the 1966 *Joint Statement on Government of Colleges and Universities* and, at the same time, allow for an honestly accountable presidency.

BACKGROUND

Colleges and universities are essentially corporations formed for the purpose of education. Like other institutions that serve the public good, they are unique in that they are governed primarily by lay persons who are not educators and who serve without compensation. Such has been the case since the seventeenth century.

The lay governing board is not unique to America, but was first practiced in Italy, The Netherlands, and Scotland. In England, on the other hand, Oxford and Cambridge were governed by senior faculty who let the institutions decay to the point that the universities had to call for government intervention to

---

*Not on AGB list.

address their problems. Since that time, no English universities have been established without lay boards. In German universities, the professoriate was subject to such intense polarization that they were an easy mark for the Nazis.

Today lay control has come to be the preferred form of governance in higher education—ideally, not so closely involved that it can't change (faculty) and not so far that it can be too quickly changed by the shifting winds of politics (government). The modifier that has generally worked well over the years is the acceptance by governing boards of the practices of academic freedom and shared governance. Academic freedom guarantees the faculty the right to teach and interpret their subjects without interference, and shared governance gives the faculty the privilege of participating in institutional decision-making. The main problems in higher education lie in the interpretation of these two practices. Governing boards have increasingly granted to faculty, staff, and students prerogatives that were traditionally privileges to be granted by the president.

At first these democratized governance conditions appeared in a few institutions, but through the years their numbers multiplied. Eventually their proponents moved into the mainstream of higher education and their positions began to be reflected in the programs and publications of national organizations. AGB is the most obvious example at the national level, and many believe that AGB often represents the interest of the faculty to the detriment of the president and the board.

Whether these charges are true or not is certainly debatable, and the following discussion of trustee responsibilities attempts to suggest a range of possible interpretations. My own position is that AGB has been the most responsive national organization in higher education, and, rather than withdrawing, institutions whose leaders are dissatisfied should actively participate in the organization and press for their particular positions. I feel confident that these institutions will be heard and recognized.

1. APPOINTING THE PRESIDENT

Failing in this, the most important responsibility of the governing board, is among the major problems in American higher education today. In general, the appointment process has become so compromised that it is bound to produce a questionable appointment: the wrong committee is appointed, outside consultation is not used, searches take too long, referencing is done poorly, and confidentiality is breached. Once the wrong committee has been appointed, nothing can be done to correct the course (short of abolishing the committee).

Without deliberation, many governing boards have abrogated their responsibility for presidential appointment by granting a disproportionate role in the process to faculty. In many institutions faculty make up a majority of the search committee and play the major role in developing the search policy and directing the search process. In a number of cases, faculty committees screen *all* presidential candidates before any are reviewed by the board. Many institutions have modifications of this usually unfortunate practice.

As the role of the board has become increasingly less important in the presidential appointment process, the status of the presidential office has declined, academic standards have gone down, public confidence has diminished, and higher education has been unable to make the changes necessary to restore itself. If there is to be a restoration process, it must start with the presidential appointment procedure. This procedure should be, at least initially, under the exclusive authority of the board.

The key features to an effective and efficient presidential search are:

1. the appointment of consultants, especially a general consultant before the appointment of the search committee;
2. the membership of the search committee;
3. the right search process;
4. complete confidentiality from beginning to end;
5. an institutional review or audit;
6. an emphasis on referencing over interviews with the search committee or the board;
7. a compensation package tailored to the needs of the final candidate;

2. EVALUATING THE INSTITUTION

Unless the governing board or a newly appointed president insists, institutions are rarely evaluated by external review. In part, this may be due to a lack of emphasis on the part of AGB, which speaks of the importance of institutional assessment but does not give it a place on its list of governing board responsibilities. The good condition of the institution is the primary trust of the governing board. Accreditation does not do the job, for it is primarily a confirmation of minimum standards. Most institutions go unexamined by others except for those whose interests (faculty and staff) imply the highest possible evaluation.

While there are indices a board can follow to determine the general condition of the institution (trends in enrollment, standardized test scores, external support, faculty credentials and publications, and recency of curriculum changes), these are contextual and often imprecise as well as incomplete. Most boards never have a full expert and objective evaluation of their institutions; they simply assume that things are good (or bad) and proceed from there. The *only* way a board can get a reasonably accurate reading of the condition of the institution is to commission an outside "authority" who assembles a team that examines the entire institution.

No board should undertake a presidential search without a thorough assessment of its present condition in order to intelligently determine its needs for the next presidency. With extraordinary exceptions, most boards seem to believe that a search committee can accurately determine the condition of the institution and its present needs, or that a search consultant can come in for a quick assessment and the job is done. The idea is ludicrous.

In one distinguished university, the board had a feeling that the institution had been resting on its laurels and might be slipping. During a presidential vacancy, the board engaged an outside consultant who conducted a complete evaluation of the institution. The evaluation concluded that the board was correct—the institution was slipping. The search committee and its search consultant appropriately adjusted the presidential selection criteria, and a president was appointed who very probably would not have met the initial criteria.

It is also increasingly common for newly appointed presidents to commission an outside institutional evaluation if the board has not already had it done. The institution is then able to both unearth and address issues and conditions that otherwise might continue unattended or that might inspire unproductive conflict if initiated by the new president. Sitting presidents and boards use institutional evaluations for the same purposes, or as a check on how things are going and where the institution should place its new initiatives. Most importantly, it is a basic responsibility of the governing board to ensure that periodic institutional evaluations be conducted in order that the board can more nearly determine its effectiveness.

3. ASSESSING BOARD POLICIES

The policies of a board may change through practice and amendment, or a board may make no alterations in policy in spite of changing institutional needs. Both conditions set the stage for serious problems.

A board can prevent these problems by insisting on a periodic review of its bylaws and practices. An outside consultant is clearly in the best position to conduct an objective review, but the important point here is that the board commission regular and complete reviews of all governance documents and board policies.

A typical occurrence may be, although the board's original policies called for a clear relationship between the board and the president, over the years these policies became muddied by practices that dramatically reduce the authority and the accountability of the president. The institution drifts into a contentious torpor in which no one is happy and things continue from bad to worse.

In one instance, a board went through four presidents in nine years before realizing that the primary fault was in its policies and practices rather than in the presidents who had been deposed. In another institution, the governing board was able to secure its leading presidential candidate only because its bylaws had been reviewed and its policies revised. The candidate would not have taken the position otherwise.

A board should commission an outside review of its governance documents at least every five years. The full board should discuss the resulting recommendations and consider changes that may be appropriate. Unfortunately, AGB has merely pointed out this key responsibility and not highlighted it.

4. SUPPORTING THE PRESIDENT

The board should give the president both psychological and substantive support. Both are essential and often overlapping, but are too often unappreciated or taken for granted by a board. The result can be an unhappy and less effective president. This can lead to shorter presidential tenures.

When a board appoints a president, it accepts the responsibility of being—and being perceived to be, both on and off campus—solidly behind that president. Board members should resolve any reservations behind closed doors, either in one-on-one meetings or in executive sessions. A board must be prepared for the controversy that is a certain by-product of a dynamic president. Even the most mundane circumstances often involve conflicting positions that only the president can resolve. However the issues are resolved, some people are bound to be unhappy.

If the board had properly delegated to the president the responsibility and authority for running the institution, the president would be perceived to be the agent of the board with its complete mandate. If faculty and others sense that the board, or even certain members of the board, do not back the president, these uncertain relationships create role confusion and unnecessary and unproductive conflict. Finally the president becomes a scapegoat for all parties and is judged ineffective. Every president deserves the opportunity to succeed or fail on his or her own merits and not because of ambiguous or wrong board practices and policies.

It is also important that the board tell the president, from time to time, that it appreciates that things are going well, if in fact they are. The board should make these kinds of affirming statements in official board meetings as well as in less formal settings.

The second dimension of presidential support is substantive, that is, presidential compensation. Too often the board takes it for granted that presidential compensation is sufficient. Indeed, compensation is often an afterthought in presidential searches, seriously considered only when the board is about to negotiate with the first-choice candidate. Although this would be hard to document, it's surely true that countless interested candidates have been lost at this point.

The astute board will have a special compensation committee charged with thoughtfully attending to the needs of the president, and this not only includes salary and other prerequisites (everything from special annuities to rabbi contracts), but also the president's physical and emotional health. Today many boards insist that their presidents take annual vacations and have regular physical examinations. Some institutions engage executive compensation firms to conduct compensation studies and make recommendations.

But too often boards merely look at last year's package, do a quick review of national compensation studies (which are invariably misleading), and then decide what to do for the president. Suffice it to say, many good presidents are lost in this way. Indeed, I would hazard that more able presidents are either lost or decide to decline the position for reasons of compensation than for any other single reason. Although presidents and presidential candidates rarely admit to a board that compensation is the primary reason they leave or decline a position, in time this truth comes out.

---

5. REVIEWING THE PERFORMANCE OF THE PRESIDENT

Although this responsibility is second in importance only to appointing the president, most boards do a poor job of it. Either they do no presidential evaluation or they do it poorly. In spite of the importance of presidential evaluation, it is infinitely better for a board to do nothing than to do a poor one. This is another area where AGB materials are misleading.

Informal evaluation may or may not include contacts with faculty and others by the board. Evaluations that include faculty lead to less effective presidents, even if the president passes with flying colors. The process itself diminishes the presidential office. According to leadership research, it is far better for the board to interview *no one*, confining its activities to an annual evaluation of the president according to mutually acceptable objectives in an executive session.

Approximately every five years, the board should commission a more formal presidential evaluation to be done by an external authority. The selection of this person is most important. A poor choice can also lead to a diminished presidency. The board should consult the president and gain his or her concurrence before appointing a consultant. The key to an effective formal evaluation is that members of the faculty and staff *are not* systematically included in the process. In no way must the people gain the impression that the president is up for vote. In most instances during recent years, this has been the case.

Both informal and formal evaluations can be invaluable to both the board and the president. The board should, in return, invite the president to express opinions about its conduct. Evaluations of record provide for the president and the board a regular assessment that makes for thoughtful and reasonable consideration of their mutual effectiveness.

6. REVIEWING THE MISSION OF THE INSTITUTION

At least every five years, the board should ask the president to commission a review of the objective of the institution that will be presented to the board for discussion. That is, the board should not do it but should ensure that it is done.

The review should answer these kinds of questions: What is our mission? Do we teach different subjects from other institutions? If so, at what levels? How can we improve the curriculum?. . . .the student body?. . . .the faculty?. . . .our overall effectiveness?. . . .our efficiency? Do we have obligations to special interests and groups?

The president should include faculty, staff, and students in this mission review, which becomes increasingly refined as it proceeds through the institution. Finally, the president presents the reviewed and possibly revised mission to the board.

Once the board has reviewed and approved the mission, it should be distributed widely to the campus community. This gives faculty, staff, and students the opportunity to invest or reinvest in the grander mission of the institution and to more nearly define their own roles in these terms.

7. APPROVING LONG-RANGE PLANS

Long-range planning is the strategy for achieving the mission of the institution. "It is a process that articulates institutional mission, weighs external opportunities and threats, gauges internal strengths and weaknesses, and determines appropriate action" (Shirley, 1988). The long-range plan should be written and updated annually. The long-range plan is prepared by the president in consultation with administrative associates and faculty, staff, and students. In some public institutions, state officials are also included in long-range planning, but in most instances this practice has not proven particularly fruitful.

If there are differences regarding the long-range plan, the board should not reconcile them (as advocated by AGB). It is the president who should consider the differences and make the final decision. While the president should be bound to explain to the board the opposing sides in an unresolved conflict, the board should publicly support whatever decision the president makes. Except in the most unusual circumstances, the board itself should never be the final arbitrator. This would diminish the legitimate position of its agent, the president. Should there be compelling arguments on both sides of a conflict, the president will probably seek counsel informally from key members of the board.

8. OVERSEEING THE EDUCATIONAL PROGRAM

The curriculum and research activities are the core of the institution and the basic trust of the board; the test against which all things should be measured. Unfortunately, the academic program has also become the most nearly sacrosanct area of the institution as faculties have assumed, and been given by boards and presidents, an ever more inviolate role. Despite the fact that this incongruous and puzzling condition is fairly recent (this century), it is now considered in many important quarters as being a part of the historic fabric of American higher education.

How can a board maintain its trust if it denies both its primary and accountable agent, the president, any real authority over what the institution does? Today institutional bylaws frequently contain passages like the following, which deprive presidents of any but a ceremonial role in the academic program:

> The formulation and implementation of academic policy shall be the responsibility of the faculty. It shall discharge this authority under the Board of Trustees.

Or this, which effectively eliminates both the president and the board:

> These by–laws may be altered, amended, or repealed by the Board only after consultation with the principal legislative body of the University [the faculty] . . . .

It is as if the reconstructionist professors of the early 1900s had won the day after all. Surely it is true that some boards and some presidents could ignore the views of faculty, but it is equally true that institutions controlled by academics are not democratic either. Any change in such institutions is all but impossible. To give the faculty complete authority over academic matters is comparable to turning the government over to the bureaucrats, the Defense Department over to the military, or religious institutions over to the clergy. The answer is to fashion a form of campus-shared governance in which everyone affected by decisions, especially the faculty, have a voice in their making.

The curriculum and research activities *should* be the primary responsibility of the faculty; that is what they are appointed to do. There is a vast difference between responsibility, authority, and *accountability.* While a faculty can assume all of the responsibility and the greater measure of the authority, it can assume virtually *none* of the accountability. This is the reason that faculty-driven institutions become paralyzed.

It is the president and the board who are accountable for the conduct of the institution. The president, as the delegate of the board, takes a calculated risk in granting authority to the faculty for which they cannot be held accountable. While this is advisable in the case of academic affairs, it nonetheless remains true that the president and the board, and ultimately those to whom the institution is dedicated, pay the price for any academic misconduct. The collective faculty cannot be held accountable for anything.

The board should not meddle with the curriculum. It should be concerned with such questions as the comparative emphasis on teaching and research, the qualifications of students who should be admitted, and the general content of the curriculum. While academic freedom for the faculty embraces both the courses to be taught and how they are interpreted, the board should be informed of methods of evaluation and their results. The board should make the final decision regarding the addition or elimination of academic programs.

The board retains final authority for academic matters, but it delegates to the president virtually everything but that final authority. On academic matters, the president recommends and the board listens very thoughtfully, objecting only in extreme cases. The board should regularly review academic matters, including the curriculum.

---

9. ENSURING FINANCIAL SOLVENCY

Money is the board responsibility to which no one objects. While others want to run the institution, they quickly and confidently turn to the board for financial support. Board members are generally more comfortable dealing with financial and business affairs. It is not surprising that most boards spend a disproportionate amount of time on finances and related areas. In my experience as a board member and a college president, I never saw a board that was not too involved in financial affairs (excluding fund raising) and not insufficiently informed about the academic program of the institution.

The board must see that the budget is balanced, and that in the last analysis income equals expenditures. The board must also be concerned about the property of the institution and the investment of institutional monies. Some administrators tend to let deficits accumulate in the hope of a brighter tomorrow, rather than making cutbacks in programs or personnel. In prosperity, institutions are usually less attentive to costs and expenses. In both instances, there is a need for close board review.

When a budget is out of balance, trustees must find a way to correct the condition. This can be done in two ways: reducing costs and/or increasing income. An institution can increase its income by adding students, engaging in institutional entrepreneurial activities, increasing tuition and fees, and launching fund-raising efforts. Many believe that there has been a disproportionate emphasis on increasing tuition and fees during recent years, but there is no real evidence that fee increases hurt an institution. The counterpoint is to increase financial aid for those who cannot afford the tuition increases. It is surely more difficult to reduce costs and to raise private support. Entrepreneurial activities on the part of colleges and universities are increasingly subject to question.

Raising money for the institution is a basic board responsibility that can only receive proper due by frequent reminders from board leadership. In this case, the initiative is the board's rather than the president's. The traditional mandate that a board member would provide either "work, wealth, or wisdom" has been replaced with today's order to "give, get, or get off." Every board member should be concerned with raising financial support for the institution. Not only should every board member contribute, but board members should ask for additional ways to be involved in fund raising for the institution. Board members should be optimistic in the face of difficulty and recognize the truism that, to a great measure, "People give because of who asks them." When staff of the institution ask for involvement, it is the obligation of every member of the board to respond enthusiastically, regardless of whether or not they "like to raise money."

In addition to having an experienced chief development officer, the following are generally accepted as the characteristics of an effective fund-raising program:

— amount allocated for fund raising;
— at least four professionals in fund raising and recent additions;
— relatively high endowment;
— emphasis on capital gifts (nonoperational funds);
— emphasis on planned giving, prospect research, and annual fund;

- trustee involvement;
- active trustee development planning;
- presidential involvement (between fifteen and forty solicitations annually);
- use of outside counsel;
- size of mailing list;
- significant annual increase of giving.

Successful fund raising can only be accomplished with a strong, united board and presidential support. If these conditions exist, a top staff can be appointed and nourished and impressive results achieved.

---

10. PRESERVING INSTITUTIONAL INDEPENDENCE

One of the great sources of strength for American colleges and universities has been their independence or, to put it more accurately, their relative independence from outside control, that gives them the freedom to pursue their own truth. By nature a college or university is controversial as well as important, and outside groups often try to use an institution for special purposes (political, bureaucratic, personal, business, etc.). Because it is also vulnerable, an institution needs a strong board to protect its independence. The very knowledge that such a board exists is usually sufficient to ward off the contractor who wants special consideration, the influential citizen who wants special admission treatment for his son, the important elected official who feels that the institution should more nearly represent her political interest or who needs a job for a friend, the government bureaucrat with a penchant for running colleges and universities, or the donor who wants to attach inappropriate conditions to a major gift.

A key role of a college or university is to take exception with the conventional wisdom, from both the left and the right. The institution is a sanctuary for the expression of ideas, and the board must insist on policies that protect the institution from extremists from both inside and outside. While the university ensures the right to express ideas that may be unpopular, it is also bound to see that the laws are enforced. For instance, if, in the course of dissent, students or staff violate the duly-constituted law, the institution is bound to have them prosecuted. There can be no institutional forgiveness for reasons of youth, motivation, or sympathy. In the case of civil disobedience, if the student or staff member has the right to violate the law the institution has the obligation to see that the law is enforced. And it is the responsibility of the board to see that it is done.

11. REPRESENTING THE INSTITUTION AND THE PUBLIC

Colleges and universities are bound to be controversial, and the duty of a trustee is to explain, defend, and enhance the institution under this condition. A college or university that isn't at times controversial isn't worth the name. Truth is never absolute and rarely comfortable, and as the primary function of a college or university is to pursue and interpret the truth, a board should never find comfort in a smooth course.

It is the trustees who interpret the campus to the external community and provide the legitimate link to those who might otherwise object. It is easy to sing the praises of an institution in ivy-covered moments; it is quite another thing to defend it when it is in trouble. To do these things effectively, trustees must be informed about the institution—they must know its mission, its programs, and its plans.

Trustees may at times be called upon to defend things they do not support, such as the appearance on campus of a controversial speaker or the performance of an avant garde play. These situations are the test of the effective trustee. The time for questioning institutional practice is in the privacy of a board meeting. In public, the trustee either champions the institution or supportively states that the chair of the board or the president will speak on that particular issue.

Conversely, trustees represent the views of the external public to the staff and, in so doing, enhance the breadth and view of the institution. Representing society to the institution is an important trustee responsibility, as societal changes occur, institutions are invariably reluctant to change. Colleges and universities are no exception. Colleges often tend to live in relative isolation or to feel that the outside holds questionable values and is unworthy of serious consideration. In a shrinking and high-tech world, colleges and universities are woefully slow to embrace the importance of requiring foreign languages, full computer literacy, or fully-integrated student bodies. Trustees cannot themselves make these changes but they can insist that officials of the institution be aware of the academic and management implications of the greater society.

12. SERVING AS A COURT OF APPEAL

On rare occasions a board of trustees may be pressed to sit in judgment over an institutional dispute. We have become a litigious society, and often staff or faculty or students will question judgments against them. Contrary to the conventional wisdom (AGB) on this subject, the board should support the president *pro forma.* If the issue is pressed, let it be in the courts of law. To do otherwise not only reduces the legitimacy of the president but establishes a most unfortunate precedent.

This kind of situation can best be prevented if the board insists on well-publicized procedures regarding faculty appointment, promotion, and tenure, and expected student conduct. As potential problems develop, it is wise for the president to consult informally with the board chair.

13. DETERMINING BOARD PERFORMANCE

Once a year the board in executive session should ask the president, "How are we doing?" Some boards appoint a board committee (not the executive committee) to annually consider the performance of the board. This might be the presidential compensation committee (if it is not the executive committee); this committee also evaluates the president. This would assure that the same group considers the performance of both the board and the president.

At least every five years, the board should engage an outside consultant to help answer questions regarding the performance of the board. While board performance is usually addressed in an institutional evaluation and in a presidential review, the board chair should specifically ask the outside evaluator to assess the board itself.

In sum, this presentation enables each important segment of the university community—board, president, and faculty—to play its proper and effective role in governing the institution. At the same time, the interpretation of these responsibilities allows the president to play the key role in the institutional leadership and to be fairly measured in that performance.

Epilogue

If at this point the reader is still inclined to be skeptical, I suggest a review of the history of higher education in an effort to find exceptions to the presence of a strong, empowered president in the development of any successful college or university. Conversely, try to find any distinguished institution in formative or troubled years that continued control by its faculty, that in times of difficulty survived without an empowered president. Participation, yes, but final authority cannot be given to a faculty, and governing boards cannot administer, because a collective—saving full bankruptcy—cannot be held accountable. Only completely secured institutions can afford collegial presidents who can only continue until the next crisis.

As leaders, presidents have been the key dimension in the history of American colleges and universities. They will also be a crucial part of their good future. Above all, it is the responsibility of governing boards to provide conditions that will enable presidents to be honestly held accountable for the conduct of their institutions. It will be at that point, and only then, that our institutions will be able to move.

Appendixes

A. INITIAL LETTER FROM BOARD TO PRESIDENTIAL SEARCH COMMITTEE

Presidential Search Committee

Role of the Committee

The role of the committee is to assist the Board of (institution) in identifying and screening qualified candidates for the position of president and to advise the Board regarding the selection of highly qualified and acceptable persons for the position.

Specific Responsibilities of the Committee

1. To assess the present condition of the university and to develop a profile of desired characteristics and qualifications for the next president.
2. To develop an advertisement for the position.
3. To organize and promote an active search for qualified candidates for the position. This involves not only the placement of appropriate notices of the vacancy but, most importantly, a vigorous search for outstanding candidates from all appropriate sources with special attention to seeking qualified women and minority candidates.
4. To review carefully all applicants and nominees in accordance with the profile and needs of the University.
5. To recommend to the Board by (date), the names of no less than two nor more than three candidates, without preference.

Procedural Guidelines

1. The search committee is established to assist and advise the Board.

2. The search process must be conducted within the letter and spirit of established affirmative action and equal employment policies and procedures.

3. Above all, the search committee should establish procedures that insure confidentiality regarding its work and the names of candidates. *Only the committee chair, or his/her designate, should make public statements regarding the search.*

4. The search process should conducted in a manner that will enable the appointment of a highly qualified person to the position. It also should provide the basis for a successful transition into office for the person selected.

B. CHECKLIST FOR THE SEARCH PROCESS

Steps in an Efficient and Effective Presidential Search Process (four to five months)

Weeks 1 and 2

Points one through eleven below can be done before the first search committee meeting and usually take from two to six weeks, depending on time constraints.

_____ 1.   Vacancy.

_____ 2.   Employment of general consultant who speaks to board or executive committee.

_____ 3.   Chair of search committee appointed by board (usually board chair).

_____ 4.   Appoint search consultant (consider three to six firms, both profit and non-profit; interview at least three; cost from 20 percent to 33 1/3 percent of first year's salary, or flat rate plus expenses). Have general consultant sit in on interviews.

_____ 5.   Consider an outside institutional review to get an objective assessment of the institution; to define appropriate characteristics of the next president; to inspire the interest of top candidates.

_____ 6.   Begin institutional review.

_____ 7.   Consider an outside compensation study.

_____ 8.   Budget ($25,000-$150,000 and more). Be generous, it will be worth it at twice the cost.

_____ 9.   Search committee appointed by board with distinct majority of board members (seven to fifteen members: nine preferred).

_____ 10.   Vacancy posted in *The Chronicle of Higher Education, The New York Times, The Wall Street Journal*, significant minority and women's publications, et al.

_____ 11.   Draft charge to search committee.

_____ 12.   News release or press conference or both announcing general time frame, stressing confidentiality, and other conditions of the search.

Week 3

_____ 13.   *First meeting of the search committee.*

_____ 14.   Opening statement by committee chair. Present charge from board: time frame-four to five months, but announce six or more, number of candidates to be recommended without preference, confidentiality, et al. Appointment of secretary, clerical assistance, permanent meeting and office space; stress confidentiality.

_____ 15. Blood oath by committee to confidentiality. Chair appointed as single spokesperson.

_____ 16. Presentation by general consultant.

_____ 17. Timetable adopted (median 7.5 months; most take entirely too long; a thorough search can be done in four to five months).

_____ 18. Presentation by outgoing president (and perhaps others).

_____ 19. Presentation by affirmative action officer.

_____ 20. Establish communication process with candidates and others (all through separate search office over signature of chair of search committee).

_____ 21. General consultant provides sample letters to be sent inviting nominations from significant persons in higher education.

_____ 22. Consider public hearing (faculty, staff, students, alumni leaders, community leaders, any interested parties).

_____ 23. Invite search consultant into committee meeting.

Between Meetings

_____ 24. Applications begin to arrive.

_____ 25. Letters of acknowledgement sent to candidates asking for three to six references.

_____ 26. Preliminary sort of applications conducted by search consultant and search committee chair.

_____ 27. All committee members encouraged to visit search office and study candidate files.

_____ 28. Public hearing conducted day before second search committee meeting.

_____ 29. *Institutional Review* completed.

Week 9

_____ 30. *Second search committee meeting.*

_____ 31. Review by chair and consultant (stress confidentiality).

_____ 32. Discussion of *Institutional Review*. Copies, with letters, sent to important persons soliciting nominations and top candidates.

_____ 33. Committee reviews candidate files (allow one and a half to two hours of private time at beginning of the meeting to review the top thirty to forty).

_____ 34. Committee discusses candidates. Reduces list to fifteen to twenty.

_____ 35. Committee members receive referencing assignments.

Between Meetings

_____ 36. Referencing by committee and consultants while continuing to accept nominations and develop candidate list.

Week 12

_____ 37. *Third search committee meeting*

_____ 38. Review by chair and consultant of new candidates and prospects and update on others (stress confidentiality).

_____ 39. Discuss referencing on top fifteen to twenty and re-consider temporarily discarded and new candidates.

_____ 40. Reduce list to seven to ten candidates to be interviewed.

_____ 41. Other candidates kept in reserve. (No candidates are dismissed until the search is complete.)

Between Meetings

_____ 42. Further telephone checks, personal interviews, and possible site visits by consultant and/or committee members. (Usually consultant does a better job.)

Week 14

_____ 43. *Fourth search committee meeting.*

_____ 44. Review by chair and consultant (stress confidentiality).

_____ 45. Interview top seven to ten candidates, preferably off-campus, using forms prepared from the institutional review.

_____ 46. Committee discusses candidates. Reduces list to three to five finalists for off-campus interviews (three are preferred).

Between Meetings

_____ 47. Further referencing and possible site visits by consultant.

Week 16

_____ 48. *Final interviews with board.* (At this point there may also be non-public, confidential interviews with a special faculty screening committee shortly preceeding the board interviews.)

All interviews should be conducted off-campus and use the same interview forms.

_____ 49. Evaluation of final candidates by board, possibly including additional interviews. The general consultant and the search consultant may or may not be present. (If no candidate is acceptable, return to step forty-one or step ten).

After Board Decision

_____ 50. Job offer is made immediately with precise terms of employment, evaluation, separation. If rejected, return to step forty-eight.

_____ 51. New appointee informs present employer.

_____ 52. Other finalists quickly informed.

_____ 53. Public announcement with press release approved by president-designate followed by press conference.

_____ 54. Release sent to other candidates.

_____ 55. Files closed.

_____ 56. Financial records audited.

_____ 57. Files stored.

C. PRESS RELEASE (FOR RELEASE AFTER THE FIRST SEARCH COMMITTEE MEETING)

Date

Place

(name of institution)'s Presidential Search committee will hold a public hearing to give interested parties an opportunity to speak on the needs of the college/university as they relate to the appropriate characteristics of the next president. (name), Chair of the Search Committee, said "We believe that a public hearing will provide valuable information as we develop criteria for (name of institution)'s next president."

The hearing will convene at 1:00 p.m., (day/date) in (place). Persons desiring to make presentations should register by calling (search secretary and phone).

For more information, contact (name/title/phone).

D. ADVERTISEMENT FOR POSITION

PRESIDENT
INSTITUTION
Address

The Board of (<u>institution</u>) announces the search for a President to be named in the fall of (<u>year</u>) who will assume office in (<u>month, year</u>). Nominations and expressions of interest should be forwarded to:
<u>(Chair of Search Committee)</u>
<u>(Address)</u>

(<u>Institution</u>) is an Equal Opportunity/Affirmative Action Institution.

E. LETTER TO PERSONS AND ORGANIZATIONS INVITING NOMINATIONS

Dear President:

The Board is seeking a president for (name of institution) who will be named in (year) and assume office in the summer of (year).

We are requesting that you assist us in filling this position. We will be grateful for your nomination of one or more candidates. You may assure any nominees that the search will be conducted in professional confidence. Please write to:

(name, address: Search Committee Chair)

We appreciate your assistance.

Sincerely,

Chair,
for the committee

F. ANNOUNCEMENT TO THE MEMBERS OF THE UNIVERSITY COMMUNITY INVITING NOMINATIONS

To: Members of the University Community

As you know, a search committee has been established by the Board to recommend, seek out, and review candidates for the presidency of (institution). The committee is composed of nine members: five members of the Board, two faculty members, one student, and one alumnus.

Specifically, our charge is to recommend to the Board the names of no less than two nor more than three candidates. Although we have until (date), we plan on completing this assignment by (date). This should provide for a smooth and orderly transition and the president-elect would assume office during the summer of (year).

We invite you to participate in identifying outstanding candidates. Please address nominations to (search secretary) at (search office address). Be assured that all candidates will receive our thoughtful consideration.

Candidates should have demonstrated excellence in academic and administrative leadership, or their equivalent in other areas of endeavor, good interpersonal skills, management ability, and be a profoundly committed, articulate, energetic, and strong leader. They must have an appreciation for the role of private support (fund raising) and possess a tested, extraordinary ability to represent the college/university to its many publics and to attract the enthusiastic support of the external community.

We are committed to the appointment of an outstanding president at (institution) and will spare no energy or action in that process.

Sincerely,

Chair
Presidential Search Committee
(add names of committee members)

G. LETTER TO CANDIDATES WHO HAVE APPLIED

Date

Name and address of applicant

Dear _____ :

We are pleased to include you as a candidate for the Presidency of (<u>institution</u>). Would you forward us an up-to-date resumé and include the names, addresses, and telephone numbers of at least three references. Unless otherwise directed by you, it is our intention to keep all information regarding your candidacy confidential. The information will, of course, be shared with all members of the search committee and our consultants.

The search committee hopes to make its recommendation to the Board by (<u>date</u>).

Sincerely,

Chair, Search Committee

enclosure: Charge to the Search Committee

H. LETTER TO CANDIDATES WHO HAVE BEEN NOMINATED

Date

Name and address of person who has been nominated

Dear _____ :

You have been nominated as a candidate for President of (institution). Assuming your interest in becoming a more serious candidate, please forward us an up-to-date resumé and include the names, addresses, and telephone numbers of at least three references. Unless otherwise directed by you, it is our intention to keep all information regarding your candidacy confidential. The information will, of course, be shared with all members of the search committee and our consultants.

The search committee hopes to make its recommendation to the Board by (date).

Sincerely,

Name, Chair
Search Committee

enclosure: Charge to Search Committee

I. LETTER TO PERSONS MAKING NOMINATIONS

Date

Name, address

Dear _____ :

Thank you for suggesting (<u>nominee</u>) as a possible candidate for the position of president at (<u>name of institution</u>). We will contact him/her in the near future and encourage his/her interest in the position.

Thank you for your interest in (<u>name of institution</u>).

Sincerely,

Name, Chair
Presidential Search Committee

J. LETTER TO APPLICANTS

Date

Name, address

Dear _____ :

Thank you for your application for the position of president at (<u>name of institution</u>). I am enclosing a copy of a preliminary position description for your information.

Our search committee is currently developing a pool of candidates and proceeding with the initial review. Since the work of our committee will depend somewhat upon the number of credentials to be reviewed and the promptness with which materials are received, it may be several weeks before we contact you again. You should feel assured, however, we will be proceeding as efficiently as possible.

Also enclosed is a form which you are asked to complete and return, in the enclosed envelope, to our Affirmative Action Officer.

On behalf of the Search Committee, please know that we are pleased by your interest and look forward to reviewing your application.

Sincerely,

Name, Chair
Presidential Search Committee

K. LETTER TO KEY PERSONS IN REGIONAL AND NATIONAL HIGHER EDUCATION AND OTHERS IN INFLUENTIAL POSITIONS

Copies of this letter and a copy of the Institutional Review should be sent to key persons in regional and national higher education and others in influential positions.

Dear _____ :

We thought the enclosed Institutional Review would further inform you about the present condition and prospects of (name of institution). After reading it, we would be happy to hear from you about candidates you have already nominated, or others whom you feel may be particularly suited to our situation.

We believe that the (institution) presidency is a remarkable opportunity for the right person and are doing everything in our power to ensure the best possible appointment. The Board is committed, faculty and students eagerly await new leadership, and our compensation package will be competitive.

Thank you for your consideration.

Sincerely,

Chair, Search Committee

L. LETTER TO ALL ON THE TOP LIST OF CANDIDATES

Copies of this letter and a copy of the Institutional Review to be sent to all on the top list of candidates.

Dear _____ :

You are one of the persons in whom the presidential search committee is most interested. We are enclosing a recently conducted review of the university for your consideration as the search process continues.

We will contact you again in the near future.

Sincerely,

Chair, Search Committee

M. JOINT STATEMENT ON GOVERNMENT OF COLLEGES AND UNIVERSITIES

Editorial Note. The *Statement* which follows is directed to governing board members, administrators, faculty members, students, and other persons in the belief that the colleges and universities of the United States have reached a stage calling for appropriately shared responsibility and cooperative action among the components of the academic institution. The *Statement* is intended to foster constructive joint thought and action, both within the institutional structure and in protection of its integrity against improper intrusions.

It is not intended that the *Statement* serve as a blueprint for government on a specific campus or as a manual for the regulation of controversy among the components of an academic institution, although it is to be hoped that the principals asserted will lead to the correction of existing weaknesses and assist in the establishment of sound structure and procedures. The *Statement* does not attempt to cover relations with those outside agencies which increasingly are controlling the resources and influencing the patterns of education in our institutions of higher learning; e.g., the United States Government, the state legislatures, state commissions, interstate associations or compacts, and other interinstitutional arrangements. However, it is hoped that the *Statement* will be helpful to these agencies in their consideration of educational matters.

Students are referred to in this *Statement* as an institutional component coordinate in importance with trustees, administrators, and faculty. There is, however, no main section on students. The omission has two causes: (1) the changes now occurring in the status of American students have plainly outdistanced the analysis by the educational community, and an attempt to define the situation without thorough study might prove unfair to student interests, and (2) students do not in fact presently have a significant voice in the government of colleges and universities; it would be unseemly to obscure, by superficial equality of length of statement, what may be a serious lag entitled to separate and full confrontation. The concern for student status felt by the organizations issuing this *Statement* is embodied in a note "On Student Status" intended to stimulate the educational community to turn its attention to an important need.

This *Statement* was jointly formulated by the American Association of University Professors, the American Council on Education, and the Association of Governing Boards of Universities and Colleges. In October 1966, the Board of Directors of the ACE took action by which the Council "recognizes the *Statement* as a significant step forward in the clarification of the respective roles of governing boards, faculties, and administrations," and "commends it to the institutions which are members of the Council." The Council of the AAUP adopted the "Statement," in October 1966, and it was endorsed by the Fifty-third Annual Meeting in April 1967. In November 1966, the Executive

Committee of the AGB took action by which that organization also "recognizes the *Statement* as a significant step forward in the clarification of the respective roles of governing boards, faculties, and administrations," and "commends it to the governing boards which are members of the Association."

1. Introduction

This *Statement* is a call to mutual understanding regarding the government of colleges and universities. Understanding, based on community of interest, and producing joint effort, is essential for at least three reasons. First, the academic institution, public or private, often has become less autonomous; buildings, research, and student tuition are supported by funds over which the college or university exercises a diminishing control. Legislative and executive governmental authority, at all levels, plays a part in the making of important decisions in academic policy.

If these voices and forces are to be successfully heard and integrated, the academic institution must be in a position to meet them with its own generally unified view. Second, regard for the welfare of the institution remains important despite the mobility and interchange of scholars. Third, a college or university in which all the components are aware of the interdependence, of the usefulness of communication among themselves, and of the force of joint action will enjoy increased capacity to solve educational problems.

II. The Academic Institution: Joint Effort

A. *Preliminary Considerations*

The variety and complexity of the tasks performed by institutions of higher education produce an inescapable interdependence among governing board, administration, faculty, students, and others. The relationship calls for adequate communication among these components, and full opportunity for appropriate joint planning and effort.

Joint effort in an academic institution will take a variety of forms appropriate to the kinds of situations encountered. In some instances, an initial exploration or recommendation will be made by the president with consideration by the faculty at a later stage; in other instances, a first and essentially definitive recommendation will be made by the faculty, subject to the endorsement of the president and the governing board. In still others, a substantive contribution can be made when student leaders are responsibly involved in the process. Although the variety of such approaches may be wide, at least two general conclusions regarding joint effort seem clearly warranted: (1) important areas of action involve at one time or another the initiating capacity and decision-making participation of all the institutional components, and (2) differences in the weight of each voice, from one point to the next, should be determined by reference to the responsibility of each component for the particular matter at hand, as developed hereinafter.

B. Determination of General Educational Policy

The general educational policy, i.e., the objectives of an institution and the nature, range, and pace of its efforts, is shaped by the institutional charter or by law, by tradition and historical development, by the present needs of the community of the institution, and by the professional aspirations and standards of those directly involved in its work. Every board will wish to go beyond its formal trustee obligation to conserve the accomplishment of the past and to engage seriously with the future; every faculty will seek to conduct an operation worthy of scholarly standards of learning; every administrative officer will strive to meet his charge and to attain the goals of the institution. The interests of all are coordinate and related, and unilateral effort can lead to confusion or conflict. Essential to a solution is a reasonably explicit statement on general educational policy. Operating responsibility and authority, and procedures for continuing review, should be clearly defined in official regulations.

When an educational goal has been established, it becomes the responsibility primarily of the faculty to determine appropriate curriculum and procedures of student instruction.

Special considerations may require particular accommodations: (1) a publicly supported institution may be regulated by statutory provisions, and (2) a church-controlled institution may be limited by its charter or bylaws. When such external requirements influence course content and manner of instruction or research, they impair the educational effectiveness of the institution.

Such matters as major changes in the size or composition of the student body and the relative emphasis to be given to the various elements of the educational and research program should involve participation of governing board, administration, and faculty prior to final decision.

C. Internal Operations of the Institution

The framing and execution of long-range plans, one of the most important aspects of institutional responsibility, should be a central and continuing concern in the academic community.

Effective planning demands that the broadest possible exchange of information and opinion should be the rule for communication among the components of a college or university. The channels of communication should be established and maintained by joint endeavor. Distinction should be observed between the institutional system of communication and the system of responsibility for the making of decisions.

A second area calling for joint effort in internal operation is that of decisions regarding existing or prospective physical resources. The board, president, and faculty should all seek agreement on basic decisions regarding buildings and other facilities to be used in the educational work of the institution.

A third area is budgeting. The allocation of resources among competing demands is central in the formal responsibility of the governing board, in the administrative authority of the president, and in the educational function of the faculty. Each component should therefore have a voice in the determination of short- and long-range priorities, and each should receive appropriate analyses of past budgetary experience, reports on current budgets and expenditures, and short- and long-range budgetary projections. The function of each component in budgetary matters should be understood by all; the allocation of authority will determine the flow of information and the scope of participation in decisions.

Joint effort of a most critical kind must be taken when an institution chooses a new president. The selection of a chief administrative officer should follow upon cooperative search by the governing board and the faculty, taking into consideration the opinions of others who are appropriately interested. The president should be equally qualified to serve both as the executive officer of the governing board and as the chief academic officer of the institution and the faculty. His dual role requires that he be able to interpret to board and faculty the educational views and concepts of institutional government of the other. He should have the confidence of the board and the faculty.

The selection of academic deans and other chief academic officers should be the responsibility of the president with the advice of and in consultation with the appropriate faculty.

Determinations of faculty status, normally based on the recommendations of the faculty groups involved, are discussed in Part V of this State*ment*; but it should here be noted that the building of a strong faculty requires careful joint effort in such actions as staff selection and promotion and the granting of tenure. Joint action should also govern dismissals; the applicable principles and procedures in these matters are well established.[1]

D. *External Relations of the Institution*

Anyone—a member of the governing board, the president or other member of the administration, a member of the faculty, or a member of the

---

[1] See the 1940 *Statement of Principles on Academic Freedom and Tenure (AAUP Bulletin* 64 [May 1978]: 108-12) and the 1958 *Statement on Procedural Standards in Faculty Dismissal Proceedings (AAUP Bulletin* 54 [Winter 1968]: 439-41). These statements have been jointly approved or adopted by the Association of American Colleges and the American Association of University Professors; the 1940 *Statement* has been endorsed by numerous learned and scientific societies and educational associations.

student body or the alumni—affects the institution when he speaks of it in public. An individual who speaks unofficially should so indicate. An official spokesman for the institution, the board, the administration, the faculty, or the student body should be guided by established policy.

It should be noted that only the board speaks legally for the whole institution, although it may delegate responsibility to an agent.

The right of a board member, an administrative officer, a faculty member, or a student to speak on general educational questions or about the administration and operations of his own institution is a part of his right as a citizen and should not be abridged by the institution.[2] There exist, of course, legal bounds relating to defamation of character, and there are questions of propriety.

III. The Academic Institution: The Governing Board

The governing board has a special obligation to assure that the history of the college or university shall serve as a prelude and inspiration to the future. The board helps relate the institution to its chief community: e.g., the community college to serve the educational needs of a defined population area or group, the church-controlled college to be cognizant of the announced position of its denomination, and the comprehensive university to discharge the many duties and to accept the appropriate new challenges which are its concern at the several levels of higher education.

The governing board of an institution of higher education in the United States operates, with few exceptions, as the final institutional authority. Private institutions are established by charters; public institutions are established by constitutional or statutory provisions. In private institutions the board is frequently self-perpetuating; in public colleges and universities the present membership of a board may be asked to suggest candidates for appointment. As a whole and individually when the governing board confronts the problem of succession, serious attention should be given to obtaining properly qualified persons. Where public law calls for election of governing board members means should be found to insure the nomination of fully suited persons, and the electorate should be informed of the relevant criteria for board membership.

---

[2] With respect to faculty members, the 1940 *Statement of Principles on Academic Freedom and Tenure* reads: "The college or university teacher is a citizen, a member of a learned profession, and an officer of an educational institution. When he speaks or writes as a citizen, he should be free from institutional censorship or discipline, but his special position in the community imposes special obligations. As a man of learning and an educational officer, he should remember that the public may judge his profession and his institution by his utterances. Hence he should at all times be accurate, should exercise appropriate restraint, should show respect for the opinion of others, and should make every effort to indicate that he is not an institutional spokesman."

Since the membership of the board may embrace both individual and collective competence of recognized weight, its advice or help may be sought through established channels by other components of the academic community. The governing board of an institution of higher education, while maintaining a general overview, entrusts the conduct of administration to the administrative officers, the president and the deans, and the conduct of teaching and research to the faculty. The board should undertake appropriate self-limitation.

One of the governing board's important tasks is to insure the publication of codified statements that define the over-all policies and procedures of the institution under its jurisdiction.

The board plays a central role in relating the likely needs of the future to predictable resources; it has the responsibility for husbanding the endowment; it is responsible for obtaining needed capital and operating funds; and in the broadest sense of the term it should pay attention to personnel policy. In order to fulfill these duties, the board should be aided by, and may insist upon, the development of long-range planning by the administration and faculty.

When ignorance or ill-will threatens the institution or any part of it, the governing board must be available for support. In grave crises it will be expected to serve as a champion. Although the action to be taken by it will usually be on behalf of the president, the faculty, or the student body, the board should make clear that the protection it offers to an individual or a group is, in fact, a fundamental defense of the vested interests of society in the educational institution.[3]

IV. The Academic Institution: The President

The president, as the chief executive officer of an institution of higher education, is measured largely by his capacity for institutional leadership. He shares responsibility for the definition and attainment of goals, for administrative action, and for operating the communications system which links the components of the academic community. He represents his institution to its many publics. His leadership role is supported by delegated authority from the board and faculty.

---

[3] Traditionally, governing boards developed within the context of single-campus institutions. In more recent times, governing and coordinating boards have increasingly tended to develop at the multi-campus, regional, systemwide, or statewide levels. As influential components of the academic community, these supra-campus bodies bear particular responsibility for protecting the autonomy of individual campuses or institutions under their jurisdiction and for implementing policies of shared responsibility. The American Association of University Professors regards the objectives and practices recommended in the 1966 *Statement* as constituting equally appropriate guidelines for such supra-campus bodies, and looks toward continued development of practices that will facilitate application of such guidelines in this new context. [Preceding note adopted by the Council in June 1978.]

As the chief planning officer of an institution, the president has a special obligation to innovate and initiate. The degree to which a president can envision new horizons for his institution, and can persuade others to see them and to work toward them, will often constitute the chief measure of his administration.

The president must at times, with or without support, infuse new life into a department; relatedly, he may at times be required, working within the concept of tenure, to solve problems of obsolescence. The president will necessarily utilize the judgments of the faculty, but in the interest of academic standards he may also seek outside evaluations by scholars of acknowledged competence.

It is the duty of the president to see to it that the standards and procedures in operational use within the college or university conform to the policy established by the governing board and to the standards of sound academic practice. It is also incumbent on the president to insure that faculty views, including dissenting views, are presented to the board in those areas and on those issues where responsibilities are shared. Similarly, the faculty should be informed of the views of the board and the administration on like issues.

The president is largely responsible for the maintenance of existing institutional resources and the creation of new resources, he has ultimate managerial responsibility for a large area of nonacademic activities, he is responsible for public understanding, and by the nature of his office is the chief spokesman of his institution. In these and other areas his work is to plan, to organize, to direct, and to represent. The presidential function should receive the general support of board and faculty.

V. The Academic Institution: The Faculty

The faculty has primary responsibility for such fundamental areas as curriculum, subject matter and methods of instruction, research, faculty status, and those aspects of student life which relate to the educational process. On these matters the power of review or final decision lodged in the governing board or delegated by it to the president should be exercised adversely only in exceptional circumstances, and for reasons communicated to the faculty. It is desirable that the faculty should, following such communication, have opportunity for further consideration and further transmittal of its views to the president or board. Budgets, manpower limitations, the time element, and the policies of other groups, bodies, and agencies having jurisdiction over the institution may set limits to realization of faculty advice.

The faculty sets the requirements for the degrees offered in course, determines when the requirements have been met, and authorizes the president and board to grant the degrees thus achieved.

Faculty status and related matters are primarily a faculty responsibility; this area includes appointments, reappointments, decisions not to reappoint, promotions, the granting of tenure, and dismissal, the primary responsibility of the faculty for such matters is based upon the fact that its judgment is central to general educational policy. Furthermore, scholars in a particular field or activity have the chief competence for judging the work of their colleagues; in such competence it is implicit that responsibility exists for both adverse and favorable judgments. Likewise there is the more general competence of experienced faculty personnel committees having a broader charge. Determinations in these matters should first be by faculty action through established procedures, reviewed by the chief academic officers with the concurrence of the board. The governing board and president should, on questions of faculty status, as in other matters where the faculty has primary responsibility, concur with the faculty judgment except in rare instances and for compelling reasons which should be stated in detail.

The faculty should actively participate in the determination of policies and procedures governing salary increases.

The chairman or head of a department, who serves as the chief representative of his department within an institution, should be selected either by departmental election or by appointment following consultation with members of the department and of related departments; appointments should normally be in conformity with department members' judgment. The chairman or department head should not have tenure in his office; his tenure as a faculty member is a matter of separate right. He should serve for a stated term but without prejudice to re-election or to reappointment by procedures which involve appropriate faculty consultation. Board, administration, and faculty should all bear in mind that the department chairman has a special obligation to build a department strong in scholarship and teaching capacity.

Agencies for faculty participation in the government of the college or university should be established at each level where faculty responsibility is present. An agency should exist for the presentation of the views of the whole faculty. The structure and procedures for faculty participation should be designed, approved, and established by joint action of the components of the institution. Faculty representatives should be selected by the faculty according to procedures determined by the faculty.[4]

The agencies may consist of meetings of all faculty members of a department, school, college, division, or university system, or may take the

---

[4] The American Association of University Professors regards collective bargaining, properly used, as another means of achieving sound academic government. Where there is a faculty collective bargaining, the parties should seek to assure appropriate institutional governance structures which will protect the right of all faculty to participate in institutional governance in accordance with the 1966 *Statement*. [Preceding note adopted by the Council in June 1978.]

form of faculty-elected executive committees in departments and schools and a faculty-elected senate or council for larger divisions or the institution as a whole.

Among the means of communication among the faculty, administration, and governing board now in use are: (1) circulation of memoranda and reports by board committees, the administration, and faculty committees, (2) joint ad hoc committees, (3) standing liaison committees, (4) membership of faculty members on administrative bodies, and (5) membership of faculty members on governing boards. Whatever the channels of communication, they should be clearly understood and observed.

On Student Status

When students in American colleges and universities desire to participate responsibly in the government of the institution they attend, their wish should be recognized as a claim to opportunity both for educational experience and for involvement in the affairs of their college or university. Ways should be found to permit significant student participation within the limits of attainable effectiveness. The obstacles to such participation are large and should not be minimized: inexperience, untested capacity, a transitory status which means that present action does not carry with it subsequent responsibility, and the inescapable fact that the other components of the institution are in a position of judgment over the students. It is important to recognize that student needs are strongly related to educational experience, both formal and informal. Students expect, and have a right to expect, that the educational process will be structured, that they will be stimulated by it to become independent adults, and that they will have effectively transmitted to them the cultural heritage of the larger society. If institutional support is to have its fullest possible meaning it should incorporate the strength, freshness of view, and idealism of the student body.

The respect of students for their college or university can be enhanced if they are given at least these opportunities: (1) to be listened to in the classroom without fear of institutional reprisal for the substance of their views, (2) freedom to discuss questions of institutional policy and operation, (3) the right to academic due process when charged with serious violations of institutional regulations, and (4) the same right to hear speakers of their own choice as is enjoyed by other components of the institution.

N. SAMPLE PRESIDENTIAL APPOINTMENT LETTER (PUBLIC INSTITUTION)

Name
Address

Dear Dr. _____ :

This letter shall serve as your appointment as President of (name of institution) University, on the following terms and conditions:

1.   You shall take office as President on (date) whereupon you shall become the University's Chief Executive and Academic Officer. At that time you shall also be granted tenure as a Professor of (area) in the College of (field).

2.   Your salary shall be paid from a combination of state funds and non-state funds. The state-funded salary shall be as prescribed by state policy from year to year. For the current fiscal year (dates) the President of (institution) receives $_____ from state funds. Starting (date), we anticipate a statutory increase in the range of ____%, or to approximately $_____. In addition, the Board is authorized to pay the President, out of non-state funds, a salary supplement. For the current fiscal year, the supplement is $_____. We have been advised that, for (year), we may request an increase in the supplement of an amount equal to the percentage increase in the statutory salary. Current indications are that we may also provide an additional supplement of $_____. Therefore, your total salary, from state and non-state funds, for (year) should be in the neighborhood of $_____, subject to actions of the Spring (year) General Assembly, and the final approval of the Governor.

3.   You shall have the responsibilities and authority as provided for by law and by the policies of the Board.

4.   You are required, for the convenience of the University, to reside in the University Residence. Details regarding this requirement have been supplied separately.

5.   You will be furnished an automobile for use in official business, to be paid for out of non-state funds.

6.   Your fringe benefits, such as state-funded retirement, medical, hospitalization and disability insurance, life insurance, vacation and sick leave, etc., shall be as prescribed by University policies, literature on which has been provided to you. After five years' service, you may take extended leave, with pay, for up to six months (one regular semester), or for two successive summer semesters (three months each). *This privilege will arise every five years.*

7.   You will be reimbursed for the direct, out-of-pocket costs of moving your family and household possessions from (current residence) to (future residence).

8.   You shall receive from the (name of institution) University Foundation a letter concerning a year-to-year plan for deferred additional compensation in recognition of your service to the University. *This plan for deferred additional compensation is endorsed by the Board.*

9.   Your official travel and entertainment expenses, as well as club and professional association dues, will be reimbursed according to policies of the Board.

10.   While you are encouraged to engage in professional activities that increase your stature and that of the University, you must dedicate your best efforts to the Office of the President and mission of the University. Non-university professional activities, whether for additional compensation or not, may be engaged in only upon prior approval of the Board.

11.   In the event of your resignation as President, you may either (1) terminate your total employment with the University, or (2) elect to revert to your tenured status as Professor of (area). If you revert to tenured Professor, you will join the faculty on the terms stipulated in the Faculty Handbook, with academic year salary equal to 10/12 of the state-funded President's salary. It is understood that, as President, you serve at the pleasure of the Board.

12.   As a condition to this appointment, and within twenty-one days hereof, you shall have a comprehensive physical examination by a physician mutually agreed upon and paid for by the University. This appointment shall become effective when we receive a comprehensive written report of this examination and concur that it indicates no health impairment that would prevent you from performing the duties of President. Thereafter, you shall annually submit to a similar examination, at the University's expense, and a comprehensive report from your physician shall be provided to the Board.

13.   This appointment shall otherwise become effective when officially acted upon and approved by the Board, or its Executive Committee, and when accepted by you. The provisions herein relating to your direct and indirect annual compensation are subject to law, and the approval of the Governor.

Please indicate your acceptance of this appointment by signing and returning the attached copy of this letter.

Sincerely yours,

(official signature)
Chair of the Board

Accepted and agreed to this (date)
(official signature)

O. SAMPLE FIVE-YEAR EMPLOYMENT CONTRACT

THIS AGREEMENT, made and entered into this day of (date), by and between the Board of (name of institution) , (hereinafter called the "Board" or the "College/University" and (president's name) , (hereinafter called the "President"). WITNESSETH:

WHEREAS, the Board of (name of institution) desires to employ the President as its chief administrative and executive officer, with title of "President" and,

WHEREAS, the President desires to accept such continued employment; and,

WHEREAS, the parties have agreed to the terms and conditions of such employment and desire to reduce their agreement to writing,

NOW, THEREFORE, in consideration of the promises, covenants, and agreements herein set forth, and for other good and valuable consideration, receipt of which is hereby acknowledged, the parties hereto covenant and agree as follows:

1. Terms of Employment

The Board shall employ the President for a term of five (5) years from the date hereof as its chief administrative and executive officer, with title of "President", subject to renewal or termination, as hereinafter provided. The President is hereby also granted the title "Professor of (field) with Tenure".

2. Duties

The President shall well and faithfully serve the College/University in such capacity as aforesaid, and shall at all times devote his whole time, attention, and energies to the management, superintendence, and improvement of the College/University to the utmost of his ability, and shall do and perform all such services, acts, and things connected therewith as the Board by its Bylaws have delegated to him, and which are of a nature properly belonging to the duties of a university president.

3. Compensation

The College/University shall pay the President an annual salary of $__, payable in equal sums at such intervals as the College/University has established for its payroll procedure.

4. Additional Entitlements

In addition to the annual salary, above provided, the President shall receive, and the College/University will provide the following:

a. Hospital/Medical/Surgical Insurance

The President shall be provided the benefits of the self-insured plan as provided for all faculty of the College/University, for both the President and his dependents, and pay the full premium therefor.

b. Long Term Disability Insurance

The College/University agrees to maintain two policies of Long Term Disability Insurance upon the President, and pay the premiums thereon in full, one such policy being that currently provided for members of the faculty, and one additional policy as heretofore maintained by the President individually. During any waiting period required by the policy provided for the faculty, the College/University will pay the President's salary in full, in addition to any other benefits which may be due and payable to him.

c. Workmen's Compensation Insurance

The College/University will provide Workmen's Compensation Insurance for payment of any medical expense, and compensation as provided by the laws of the State of _____ if the President suffers an injury or incurs an occupational disease arising out of and in the course of his employment. Compensability under such law is prescribed by state statute, and not by the College/University or by this Contract.

d. Retirement Fund

The President shall participate in the Retirement Fund and all required contributions thereto, as required by law, and the terms of the Plan shall be paid by the College/University.

Initially the College/University shall pay 10 percent of the President's annual salary into the Retirement Fund. This amount shall be increased at the rate of 5 percent per year until it reaches 20 percent of the President's annual salary.

e. Vacation

The President will be entitled to a vacation, with pay, of thirty (30) calendar days per year. Vacation leave not taken will be accumulated and paid for at time of termination, or at a time selected by the President, at the rate at which it is earned. However, under ordinary circumstances, the Board encourages the President to take full annual leave.

f. Sick Leave

The policy regarding sick leave, applicable to faculty and academic administrators, will be accorded to the President.

g. Residence and Expenses Connected Therewith

The College/University will provide the President with housing in the residence located at (address). The President shall furnish such furniture as he may choose to install, and if such is inadequate to completely, furnish the residence in keeping with that of a College/University President, the Board and the President will agree upon other items of furniture as may be needed and the same will be furnished by the University. The College/University shall furnish draperies and carpeting. All utilities, phone service, yard maintenance, and maintenance of the home, both outside and inside, will be paid for by the College/University. A full-time maid will be furnished at no expense to the President for use in maintaining the home so College/University guests may be properly entertained. The President and his family will be required to live in this residence furnished by the College/University. The College/ University will reimburse the President for any cost of any premiums which are paid for contents insurance on the President's furniture and personal belongings in the residence.

h. Entertainment Expenses

The College/University will provide the President with adequate budgeted funds for purposes of entertaining the guests of the College/University for carrying out the duties of the office, both on-campus and off-campus. The College/University will arrange for the payment of these expenses in a manner which is mutually acceptable to the parties.

i. Automobile

The President will be furnished with an automobile for use in carrying out the duties of the office. All expenses of this automobile, including, but not limited to, insurance, gasoline, and repairs will be paid for by the College/ University.

j. Other Faculty Privileges Not Enumerated Herein

Such other privileges and benefits accorded the faculty, not enumerated herein, will likewise be accorded to the President.

k. *Preferential Hiring Conditions for Spouse*

It is understood by the College/University that (name of spouse), spouse of the President, is a member of the tenured faculty at (name of institution) and in coming to (name of institution) with the President has surrendered valuable property rights. Therefore, the Board agrees that, in the event of the President's death before reaching retirement age, the College/University will offer (name of spouse) a teaching position at a salary to be negotiated at that time commensurate with his/her qualifications and the existing salary structure for the department where the position is offered.

1. Sabbatical Leave

The Board agrees as a result of five or more years of exemplary service, the President shall be eligible for a sabbatical leave under the following conditions, notwithstanding provision in the Faculty Handbook which may conflict herewith:

i. The President is eligible, signing a prior agreement, to a sabbatical leave of one (1) year, to be taken at the time of his choosing, providing reasonable notice of his intent to utilize such leave is given to the College/University by the President, considering all the attending circumstances. Such leave may be reserved by the President, as an option, to commence at a time of any agreed or involuntary termination of the President's services hereunder;

ii. The President shall be entitled to his full salary, and all fringe benefits payable during any such sabbatical, with the exception of the use of the President's house, which will be vacated by the President (and family) within thirty (30) days following termination, but only if terminated, unless extended by the Board;

iii. Additional sabbatical leave to that provided above, may be allowed the President, at any time by the College/University, at such time by and upon such conditions as are deemed appropriate. Such additional leave shall be granted in the sole discretion of the Board.

5. Termination

a. At least sixty (60) calendar days before the end of each year of this Agreement, the Board will conduct a performance review and evaluation of the President and shall give the President notice in writing stating the number of years it is willing to extend the Agreement, if any, beyond the years remaining in its current term established herein, and the terms upon which such extension is offered. Not later than thirty (30) calendar days following receipt of such notice, the President shall respond by stating his acceptance or rejection, or his proposed modification of the offer extended by the College/University. If agreement upon the terms of such extension is reached, a new written agreement codifying the terms thereof shall be prepared and executed by the parties. At least every four years, an evaluation of the President shall be conducted by an external authority of national reputation.

b. If no extension of the Agreement is made beyond the remaining years then existing, as above provided, this Contract shall terminate as of the first day of the last year of the term then existing.

c. This Contract may also be terminated by the parties at any time during the term, as follows:

   1. Upon the occurrence of any one of the following events:

      i. Illness or disability of the President, or any cause incapacitating him/her from the attendance to duties as President for more than one (1) year.

      ii. Termination of the President by the Board for just cause. The term "just cause" is defined as acts by the President constituting or involving incompetency, neglect, or refusal to perform his duties, or drunkenness. No termination of employment for alleged "just cause" shall occur without first giving the President notice in writing of the cause alleged, and an opportunity to be heard.

      iii. In the event the College/University terminates the President's employment for "just cause" the President shall not be entitled to any further salary or benefits following the date of such termination, unless otherwise agreed to in writing by the Board.

   2. The President may terminate this Agreement for any reason upon the giving of sixty (60) calendar days' notice, prior to the effective date of the termination. Should such notice be given, the President shall not be entitled to any further salary or benefits payable hereunder after the effective date of termination, unless otherwise agreed to in writing by the Board.

6. Construction of Agreement

The laws of the State of _____ shall govern this Agreement
(especially for public institutions)

IN WITNESS WHEREOF, the parties have executed this Agreement the day and year first above written.·

P. TAX SHELTERED ANNUITY/OTHER BENEFITS AGREEMENT

THIS AGREEMENT, made the ___ day of <u>month, year</u>, by and between <u>institution</u> of <u>location</u>, (hereinafter called the "College/University") and <u>name of president</u>, (hereinafter called the "President").

WITNESSETH:

WHEREAS, the President has been employed this same date by the College/University to serve for <u>number</u> years as its chief administrative and executive officer, with title of "President," as evidenced by a separate document entitled "Contract of Employment"; and

WHEREAS, the Board, in order to retain the services of the President, and to compensate him for the loss of benefits and other income which he experienced so he might accept employment as President, is willing to provide additional and other benefits, as set forth below; and

WHEREAS, the Board and the President have agreed to the form of such benefits to be provided to the President or to his designated beneficiaries, and desire to reduce their agreement to writing,

NOW, THEREFORE, in consideration of the promises, covenants, and agreements herein set forth, and for other good and valuable consideration, receipt of which is hereby acknowledged, the parties hereto covenant and agree as follow:

1. Retirement Privilege

The College/University agrees that the President may retire from the active and daily service of the University upon the first day of the month following his eligibility for retirement under the existent pension plan of the College/University.

2. Tax Sheltered Annuity and Tax Free Income

The College/University agrees to pay the President certain benefits outlined below:

a. The College/University will purchase and maintain for each year of this agreement a tax sheltered annuity in the maximum allowable tax-free amount of 10 percent of the total salary per year, for the sole and exclusive benefit of the President, who shall choose the plan and select such payment options and designate such beneficiaries as he may desire.

b. The College/University will pay the President an additional sum of <u>(amount)</u> for each year of this agreement in equal monthly payments or in one lump sum at the President's choosing. (This provision is especially appropriate in many public institutions with strict salary schedules. Some institutions provide this supplement as a deferred revenue plan assuming that it is tax free and meets the current needs of the President.)

c. Neither the President, nor any designated beneficiary, shall have any right to sell, assign, transfer, or otherwise convey or hypothecate the right to receive any payments from the tax deferred annuity provided in subparagraph (a.) above.

3. Term Life Insurance

The College/University will pay the premium on a policy of term life insurance upon the life of the President in the principal sum of (am ount) which will be owned by the President, and the President shall have the right to designate the beneficiary thereof. (*Some Boards prefer to provide straight life insurance plans.*)

4. Construction of the Agreement

Any payments under this Agreement shall be independent of, and in addition to, those under any other plan, program, or agreement which may be in effect between the parties hereto, or any other compensation payable to the President or to the President's designated beneficiary by the College/ University. The Agreement shall not be construed as a Contract of Employment, but shall be construed as fringe benefits given in addition to salary, nor does it restrict the right of the Board to discharge the President for just cause or the right of the President to terminate his employment.

The laws of the State of _____ shall govern this agreement. (Especially for public institutions.)

5. Amendments

This Agreement may not be altered, amended, or revoked except upon a written agreement signed by the Board and the President.

Q. A MODIFIED RABBI TRUST

Deferred Compensation Schedule

| End of Year | Contribution | | Cumulative | | |
	EOY	Cum.	Value @ 6%	Value @ 7%	Value @ 8%
1	$5,000	$5,000	$5,000	$5,000	$5,000
2	10,000	15,000	15,300	15,350	15,400
3	15,000	30,000	31,218	31,425	31,632
4	20,000	50,000	53,091	53,624	54,163
5	25,000	75,000	81,277	82,378	83,496
6	30,000	105,000	116,153	118,144	120,175
7	35,000	140,000	158,122	161,414	164,789
8	40,000	180,000	207,610	212,713	217,972
9	45,000	225,000	265,066	272,603	280,410
10	50,000	275,000	330,970	341,686	352,843

Cumulative value for each year includes accrued earnings, compounded annually, at an assumed constant rate of return shown, all on a pre-tax basis.

R. TRUST AGREEMENT

(Made for a public university but could be modified for a private institution)

THIS TRUST AGREEMENT, made and entered into as of this __ day of , 19 , between the (institution), (the "Foundation") and (name of trust company) (the "Trustee").

WITNESSETH THAT:

WHEREAS, the Foundation has entered into a contract this same date with (name of president), President of (institution) (herein to be known as the "President"), to provide certain benefits as an inducement to continue duties pursuant to an employment agreement with the College/University and to remain so employed for a period of at least (number) years, from _____, 19 to _____, 19 (usually six to ten years).

WHEREAS, the Foundation, as part of its inducement to the President, has agreed to establish a trust fund to aid it in accumulating the amounts necessary to satisfy its contractual liability to pay the President or the designated beneficiary such benefits, and

WHEREAS, the Foundation may make contributions to this trust from time to time, which contributions (if made) will be applied in payment of the Foundation's obligations to pay such benefits; and

WHEREAS, that portion of the Foundation's agreement with the President which relates to the Trust fund (also referred to herein as the "Plan") provides for the Foundation to pay all benefits thereunder from its restricted assets called "The President's Fund", and the establishment of this trust shall not reduce or otherwise affect the Foundation's continuing liability to pay benefits from such assets except that the Foundation's liability under this Trust shall be offset by actual benefit payments made by this trust; and

WHEREAS, the trust established by this Trust Agreement is intended to be classified for income tax purposes as a "grantor trust" with the result that the income of the trust be treated as income of the Foundation pursuant to Subpart E of Subchapter 3 of Chapter 1, of Subtitle A of the Internal Revenue Code of 1986, as amended (the "Code");

NOW, THEREFORE, in consideration of the mutual convenants herein contained, the Foundation and the Trustee declare and agree as follows:

Section 1. Establishment and Title of the Trust

1.1 The Foundation hereby establishes with the Trustee a trust (the "Trust"), to accept such sums of money and other property acceptable to the Trustee as from time to time may be paid or delivered to the Trustee. All such money and other property, all investments made therewith or proceeds thereof and all earnings and profits thereon that are paid to the Trustee, as provided in Section 7.1 of this Trust Agreement, less all payments and charges as authorized herein, are hereinafter referred to as the "Trust Fund". The Trust Fund shall be held by the Trustee IN TRUST and shall be dealt with in accordance with the provisions of this Trust Agreement. The Trust fund payments to the President, or the designated beneficiary, and defraying reasonable expenses of administration in accordance with the provisions of this Trust Agreement until all such payments have been made; provided, however, that the Trust fund shall at all times be subject to the claims of the creditors of the Foundation as set forth in Section 8 of this Trust Agreement.

Section 2. Acceptance by the Trustee

2.1 The Trustee accepts the Trust established under this Trust Agreement on the terms and subject to the provisions set forth herein, and it agrees to discharge and perform fully and faithfully all of the duties and obligations imposed upon it under this Trust Agreement.

Section 3. Limitation on Use of Funds

3.1 Except as provided in provisos (1), (2), and (3) of this paragraph, no part of the corpus of the Trust Fund shall be recoverable by the Foundation or used for any purpose other than for the exclusive purpose of providing payments to the President or the designated beneficiary, and defraying reasonable expenses of administration in accordance with the provisions of this Trust Agreement, until all such payments required by this Trust Agreement have been made; provided, however that (1) nothing in this Section 3.1 shall be deemed to limit or otherwise prevent the payment from the Trust Fund of expenses and other charges as provided in Sections 10.1 and 10.2 of this Trust Agreement or the application of the Trust Fund as provided in Section 6.4 of this Trust Agreement if the Trust is finally determined not to constitute a grantor trust; and (2) the Trust Fund shall at all times be subject to the claims of creditors of the Foundation as set forth in Section 8 of this Trust Agreement; and (3) provided, further that the President is able and willing to continuously serve as president of the Institution for not less than __ years, commencing with _____ , 19__ , and has not been terminated for "just cause" pursuant to his basic employment agreement with the Board. If the President elects to leave the University prior to the completion of the aforementioned __ years, or his employment is terminated during said period for "just cause", the corpus of the Trust Fund, and all accumulations thereto shall revert to the Foundation.

Section 4. Duties and Powers of the Trustee with Respect to Investments

4.1 The Trustee shall invest and reinvest the principal and income of the Trust Fund and keep the Trust Fund invested, without distinction between principal and income, in accordance with the directions of the Foundation investment guidelines as the Foundation may provide to the Trustee from time to time.

Section 5. Additional Powers and Duties of the Trustee

5.1 Subject to the provisions of Section 4.1, the Trustee shall have the following additional powers and authority with respect to all property constituting a part of the Trust Fund:

a. To sell, exchange, or transfer any such property at public or private sale for case or on credit and grant options for the purpose or exchange thereof, including call options for property held in the Trust Fund and put options for the purchase of property.

b. To participate in any plan of reorganization, consolidation, merger, combination, liquidation, or other similar plan relating to any such property, and to consent to or oppose any such plan or any action thereunder, or any contract, lease, mortgage, purchase, sale or other action by any corporation or other entity.

c. To deposit any such property with any protective, reorganization or similar committee; to delegate discretionary power to any such committee; and to pay part of the expenses and compensation of any such committee and any assessments levied with respect to any property so deposited.

d. To exercise any conversion privilege or subscription right available in connection with any such property; to oppose or to consent to the reorganization, consolidation, merger, or readjustment of the finances of any corporation, company or association, or to the sale, mortgage, pledge or lease of the property of any corporation, company, or association any of the securities of which may at any time be held in the Trust Fund and to do any act with reference thereto, including the exercise of options, the making of agreements or subscriptions, which may be deemed necessary or advisable in connection therewith, and to hold and retain any securities or other property which it may so acquire.

e. To commence or defend suits or legal proceedings and to represent the Trust in all suits or legal proceedings; to settle, compromise or submit to arbitration, any claims, debts or damages; due or owing to or from the Trust.

f. To exercise, personally or by general or limited power of attorney, any right, including the right to vote, appurtenant to any securities or other such property.

g. To borrow money from any lender in such amounts and upon such terms and conditions as shall be deemed advisable or proper to carry out the purposes of the Trust and to pledge any securities or other property for the repayment of any such loan.

h. To engage any legal counsel, including counsel to the Trustee, any enrolled actuary, or any other suitable agents, to consult with such counsel, enrolled actuary, or agents with respect to the construction of this Trust Agreement, the duties of the Trustee hereunder, the transactions contemplated by this Trust Agreement or any act which the Trustee proposes to take or omit, to rely upon the advice of such counsel, enrolled actuary or agents, and to pay its reasonable fees, expenses, and compensation.

i. To register any securities held by it in its own name or in the name of any custodian of such property or of its nominee, including the nominee of any system for the central handling of securities, with or without the addition of words indicating that such securities are held in a fiduciary capacity, to deposit or arrange for the deposit of any such securities with such a system and to hold any securities in bearer form.

j. To make, execute, and deliver, as Trustee, any and all deeds, leases, notes, bonds, guarantees, mortgages, conveyances, contracts, waivers, releases, or other instruments in writing necessary or proper for the accomplishment of any of the foregoing powers.

k. To transfer assets of the Trust Fund to a Successor trustee as provided in Section 12.4.

l. To exercise, generally, any of the powers which an individual owner might exercise in connection with property either real, personal, or mixed held by the Trust Fund, and to do all other actions that the Trustee may deem necessary or proper to carry out any of the powers set forth in this Section 5 or otherwise in the best interests of the Trust Fund, or as may be authorized by the laws of the State of _____.

Section 6. Payments by the Trustee

6.1 The establishment of the Trust and the payment of delivery to the Trustee of money or other property acceptable to the Trustee shall not vest in the President or the designated beneficiary any right, title, or interest in and to any assets of the Trust, except as otherwise set forth in this Section 6.

6.2 The Trustee shall make payment of Plan benefits to the President or to the designated beneficiary from the assets held in their respective Accounts (as defined in Section 6 hereof), in accordance with the terms and conditions, set forth in the Plan.

6.3 If the President's account is not sufficient, to make one or more payments of benefits due under the Plan to him or to the designated beneficiary in accordance with the terms of the Plan, the Foundation shall make the balance of each such payment as it falls due.

6.4   Notwithstanding anything contained in this Trust Agreement to the contrary, if at any time the Trust finally is determined by the Internal Revenue Service (IRS) not to be a "grantor trust" with the result that the income of the Trust Fund is not treated as income of the Foundation pursuant to Subpart E of Subchapter J of the code, or if a tax is finally determined by the IRS or is determined by counsel to the Trustee to be payable by the President, or by the designated beneficiaries, in respect of any vested interest in the Trust Fund prior to payment of such interest to the President or the beneficiaries, as the case may be, then the Trust shall immediately terminate and the full fair market value of the assets in the Trust, Fund shall be returned to the Foundation. The Foundation shall fully reimburse the President, or the designated beneficiary, as the case may be, for any tax liability either have incurred pursuant to the operation of this Section. For purposes of this Section, a final determination of the IRS shall be a decision rendered by the IRS which is no longer subject to administrative appeal within the IRS.

6.5 Notwithstanding any provision herein to the contrary, with respect to the President or the designated beneficiary, if the President has continued in office through the year ending _____,19_ , then the Trustee shall distribute to the President the entire sum in the trust in one lump sum.

6.6 In the event of the President's death before the expiration of the Trust Agreement, all funds in the trust on the date of death shall vest in the President's designated beneficiary, together with the payment of a pro-rated annual payment to the date of death for the year in which the death occurs. Thereafter, the entire sum in the trust shall be distributed in one lump sum to the designated beneficiary.

6.7 The Trustee shall, concurrently with the distribution of any sums from the President's Account, advise the executive office of the Foundation of the amount so paid to the President or to the designated beneficiary hereunder.

6.8 Notwithstanding anything in this Trust Agreement to the contrary, the Foundation shall remain primarily liable under the Plan to pay benefits. However, the Foundation's liability under the Plan shall be reduced or offset to the extent and by the value of any benefit payments under the Plan made from the Trust.

6.9 The Trustee shall deduct from each payment distributed under this Trust Agreement any Federal, State, or local witholding or other taxes or charges which the Trustee may be required to deduct under applicable laws.

Section 7. Funding the Trust

7.1 Amounts held for the benefit of the President (or designated beneficiary) in the Trust shall be maintained in an account (the "Account") which shall be held, administered, and accounted for separately. Records shall be maintained so that the amount held in said Account shall be identifiable at all times. The Account shall consist of, and be increased by, contributions made by the Foundation which are designated by the Foundation as the property of such Account and shall be decreased by any distributions made therefrom. The Foundation shall make contributions to such Account from time to time in accordance with the funding method provided in a separate agreement between the Foundation and the President, dated _____ , _19_ , as will permit the Trust to make payment of benefits provided by the Plan. In addition, the Trustee shall allocate and credit the New Income of the Trust to the Account of the President on the last day of each calendar year ("Allocation Date"), based on the Account balance of the President on such date.

Section 8. Trustee Responsibility Regarding Payment to the President and Beneficiaries When Foundation is Insolvent

8.1 It is the intent of the parties hereto that the Trust assets are and shall remain at all times subject to the claims of the general creditors of the Foundation. Accordingly, the Foundation shall not create a security interest in the Trust assets in favor of the President or any creditor. If the Trustee receives the notice provided for in Section 8.2 hereof, or otherwise receives actual notice that the Foundation is insolvent or bankrupt as defined in Section 8.2, the Trustee will make no further distributions from the Trust to the President, or to the designated beneficiary of the Plan, but will deliver the entire amount of the Trust assets only as a court of competent jurisdiction, or duly appointed receiver or other person authorized to act by such a court, may direct to make the Trust assets available to satisfy the claims of the Foundation general creditors. The Trustee shall resume distributions from the Trust to the President, or to the designated beneficiaries, of the Plan under the terms hereof, upon no less than thirty (30) days' advance notice to the Foundation, if it determines that the Foundation was not, or is no longer, bankrupt or insolvent. Unless the Trustee has actual knowledge of the Foundation's bankruptcy or insolvency, the Trustee shall have no duty to inquire whether the Foundation is bankrupt or insolvent.

8.2 The Foundation, through its executive officer, shall advise the trustee promptly in writing of the Foundation's bankruptcy or insolvency.

8.3 If the Trustee discontinues payments of benefits under the Plan from the Trust pursuant to Section 8.1 of this Trust Agreement and subsequently resumes such payments, the first payment to the President, or to the designated beneficiary, following such discontinuance shall include the aggregate amount of all payments which would have been made to the President, or to the designated beneficiary, in accordance with the Plan during the period of such discontinuance, less the aggregate amount of payment of benefits under the Plan made to the President, or the designated beneficiary, by the Foundation during any such period of discontinuance.

Section 9. Third Parties

9.1 A third party dealing with the Trustee shall not be required to make inquiry as to the authority of the Trustee to take any action nor be under any obligation to see to the proper application by the trustee of the proceeds of sale of any property sold by the Trustee or to inquire into the validity or propriety of any act of the Trustee.

Section 10. Taxes, Expenses, and Compensation

10.1 The Foundation shall from time to time pay taxes of any and all kinds whatsoever which at any time are lawfully levied or assessed upon or become payable in respect of the Trust fund, the income or any property forming a part thereof, or any security transaction pertaining thereto. To the extent that any taxes lawfully levied or assessed upon the trust Fund are not paid by the Foundation, the Trustee shall pay such taxes out of the Trust Fund. The Trustee shall withold Federal, State and local taxes from any payments made to the President, or to the designated beneficiary in accordance with the provisions of applicable law. The Trustee shall contest the validity of taxes in any manner deemed appropriate by the Foundation of its counsel, but at the Foundation's expense, and only if it has received an indemnity bond or other security satisfactory to it to pay any such expenses. In the alternative, the Foundation may itself contest the validity of any such taxes.

10.2 The Foundation shall pay the Trustee such reasonable compensation for its services as may be agreed upon in writing from time to time by the Foundation and the Trustee. The Foundation shall also pay the reasonable expenses incurred by the Trustee in the performance of its duties under this Trust Agreement, including brokerage commissions and fees of counsel engaged by the trustee. Such compensation and expenses shall be charged against and paid from the Trust Fund to the extent that the Foundation does not pay such compensation.

Section 11. Administration and Records

11.1 The Trustee shall keep or cause to be kept accurate and detailed accounts of any investments, receipts, disbursements, and other transactions hereunder and all necessary and appropriate records required to identify correctly and reflect accurately the interest of the President or the designated beneficiary, and all accounts, books, and records relating thereto shall be open to inspection and audit at all reasonable times by any person designated by the Foundation. All such accounts, books, and records shall be preserved for such period as the Trustee may determine, but the Trustee may only destroy such accounts, books and records after first notifying the Foundation in writing of its intention to do so, and transferring to the Foundation any of such accounts, books, and records requested.

11.2 Within thirty (30) days after the close of each calendar year, and within thirty (30) days after the removal or resignation of the Trustee or the termination of the Trust, the Trustee shall file with the Foundation, a written account setting forth all investments, receipts, disbursements and other transactions effected by it during the preceeding calendar year to the date of such removal, resignation or termination, including a description of all investments and securities purchased and sold with the cost or net proceeds of such purchases or sales and showing all cash, securities and other property held at the end of such calendar year or other period.

11.3 The Trustee shall from time to time permit an independent public accountant selected by the Foundation (except one to whom the Trustee has reasonable objection) to have access during ordinary business hours to such records as may be necessary to audit the Trustee's accounts.

11.4 As of the last day of each calendar year, the fair market value of the assets held in the Trust fund shall be determined. Within thirty (30) days after the close of each calendar year, the Trustee shall file with the Foundation the written report of the determination of such fair market value of the assets held in the Trust fund. It shall be the responsibility of the Foundation to further notify the President, or the designated beneficiary of the Trustee's report.

11.5 Nothing contained in this Trust Agreement shall be construed as depriving the Trustee, the Foundation, or the President or the designated beneficiary of the right to have a judicial settlement of the Trustee's accounts, and upon any proceeding for a judicial settlement of the Trustee's accounts or for instructions the only necessary parties thereto in addition to the Trustee shall be the foundation and the President or the designated beneficiary.

11.6 In the event of the removal or resignation of the Trustee, the Trustee shall deliver to the successor Trustee all records which shall be required by the successor Trustee to enable it to carry out the provisions of this Trust Agreement.

11.7 In addition to any returns required of the Trustee by law, the Trustee shall prepare and file such tax reports and other returns as the Foundation and the Trustee may from time to time agree.

Section 12. Removal or Resignation of the Trustee
Designation of Successor Trustee

12.1 At any time the Foundation may remove the Trustee with or without cause, upon at least sixty (60) days notice in writing to the Trustee. A copy of such notice shall be sent to the Trustee.

12.2 The Trustee may resign at any time upon at least sixty (60) days' notice in writing to the Foundation.

12.3 In the event of such removal or resignation, the Trustee shall duly file with the Foundation a written account as provided in Section 11.2 of the Trust Agreement for the period since the last previous annual accounting, listing the investments of the Trust and any uninvested cash balance thereof, and setting forth all receipts, disbursements, distributions, and other transactions respecting the Trust not included in any previous account.

12.4 Within sixty (60) days after any such notice of removal or resignation of the Trustee, the Foundation shall designate a successor Trustee qualified to act hereunder. Each such successor Trustee, during each period as it shall act as such, shall have the powers and duties herein conferred upon the Trustee, and the word "Trustee" wherever used herein, except where the context otherwise requires, shall be deemed to include any successor Trustee. Upon designation of a successor Trustee and delivery to the resigned or removed Trustee of written acceptance by the successor Trustee of such designation, such resigned or removed Trustee shall promptly assign, transfer, deliver and pay over to such Trustee, in conformity with the requirements of applicable law, the funds and properties in its control or possession then constituting the Trust Fund.

Section 13. Enforcement of Trust Agreement and Legal Proceedings

13.1 The Foundation shall have the right to enforce any provision of this Trust Agreement, and the President or the designated beneficiary of the Plan shall have the right to enforce any provision of this Trust Agreement that affects their right, title, and interest, if any, in the Trust. In any action or proceedings affecting the Trust the only necessary parties shall be the Foundation, the Trustee, and the President and the designated beneficiary of the Plan and, except as otherwise required by applicable law, no other person shall be entitled to any notice or service of process. Any judgment entered in such an action or proceeding shall to the maximum extent permitted by applicable law be binding and conclusive on all persons having or claiming to have any interest in the Trust.

Section 14. Termination and Suspension

14.1 The Trust shall terminate when all payments which have or may become payable pursuant to the terms of the Trust have been made.

Section 15. Amendments

15.1 The Foundation may from time to time amend or modify, in whole or in part, any or all of the provisions of this Trust Agreement (except Sections 1.1., 3.1, 6, 11, 12.4, 13, 14, 15, and 17) with the written consent of the Trustee, but without the consent of the President or the designated beneficiary of the Plan, provided that any such amendment shall not adversely affect the rights of the President or the designated beneficiary hereunder, or cause the Trust to cease to constitute a grantor trust as described in Section 6.4 of this Trust Agreement.

15.2 The Foundation and the Trustee shall execute such supplements to, or amendments of, this Trust Agreement as shall be necessary to give effect to any such amendment or modification.

Section 16. Nonalienation

16.1 Except insofar as applicable law may otherwise require and subject to Sections 1.1, 3.1, and 8 of this Trust Agreement, (1) no amount payable to or in respect of the President or the designated beneficiary at any time under the Trust shall be subject in any manner to alienation by anticipation, sale, transfer, assignment, bankruptcy, pledge, attachment, charge or encumbrance of any kind, and any attempt to so alienate, sell, transfer, assign, pledge, attach, charge or otherwise encumber any such amount, whether presently or thereafter payable, shall be void; and (2) the Trust Fund shall in no manner be liable for or subject to the debts or liabilities of the President of the designated beneficiary.

Section 17. Communications

17.1 Communications to the Foundation shall be addressed to the Executive Officer, (name and address of institution), provided, however, that upon the Foundation's written request, such communications shall be sent to such other address as the Foundation may specify.

17.2 Communications to the Trustee shall be addressed to (name and address of Trustee), provided, however, that upon the Trustee's written request, such communications shall be sent to such other address as the Trustee may specify.

17.3 No communication shall be binding upon the Trustee until it is received by the Trustee. No communication shall be binding on the Foundation until it is received by the Foundation. No communication shall be binding on the President or the designated beneficiary until it is received by them.

17.4 Any action of the Foundation pursuant to this Trust Agreement, including all orders, requests, directions, instructions, approvals, and objections of the Foundation to the Trustee, shall be in writing, signed on behalf of the Foundation by any duly authorized officer of the Foundation. Any action by the President or the designated beneficiary shall be in writing. The Trustee may rely on, and will be fully protected with respect to any such action taken or omitted in reliance on, any information, order, request, direction, instruction, approval, objection, and list delivered to the Trustee by the Foundation, or to the extent applicable under this Trust Agreement, by the President or the designated beneficiary.

Section 18. Miscellaneous Provisions

18.1 This Trust Agreement shall be binding upon and inure to the benefit of the Foundation and the Trustee and their respective successors and assigns and the personal representatives of individuals.

18.2 The Trustee assumes no obligation or responsibility with respect to any action required by this Trust Agreement on the part of the Foundation.

18.3 The President and the designated beneficiary shall file with the Trustee such pertinent information concerning themselves, and any other person as the Trustee shall specify, and they shall have no rights nor be entitled to any benefits under the Trust unless such information is filed by or with respect to them.

18.4 Any corporation into which the Trustee may be merged or with which it may be consolidated, or any corporation resulting from any merger, reorganization, or consolidation to which the Trustee may be a party, or any corporation to which all or substantially all the business of the Trustee may be transferred shall be the successor of the Trustee hereunder without the execution or filing of any instrument or the performance of any act.

18.5 Titles to the Sections of this Trust Agreement and included for convenience only and shall not control the meaning or interpretation of any provision of this Trust Agreement.

18.6 This Trust Agreement and the Trust established hereunder shall be governed by and construed, enforced, and administered in accordance with the laws of the State of _____ , and the Trustee shall be liable to account only in the courts of the State of _____.

18.7 This Trust Agreement may be executed in any number of counterparts, each of which shall be deemed to be the original although the others shall not be produced.

18.8 This Trust has been executed and delivered in the State of _____, and shall be construed and administered according to the laws of that State.

18.9 It is agreed that the President and the designated beneficiaries are direct third-party beneficiaries of this Trust Agreement and the terms hereof are enforceable by them.

IN WITNESS WHEREOF, this Trust Agreement has been duly executed by the parties hereto as of the day and year first above written.

                                          _____

                                          (Institution)

ATTEST: _____

                                          Foundation

_____

Witness

                                          _____

                                          Trust Company

ATTEST: _____

                                          Trustee

Bibliography

Astin, A. W., and R. A. Scherrei. *Maximizing Leadership Effectiveness.* San Francisco: Jossey-Bass, 1980.

Bass, B. M. "Individual Capability, Team Response and Productivity" in *Human Performance and Productivity,* edited by E. A. Fleischman and M. D. Dannette. New York: Erlbaum, 1981.

———. *Leadership and Performance Beyond Expectations.* New York: Macmillan, 1985.

Bennis, Warren. *Why Leaders Can't Lead.* San Francisco: Jossey-Bass, 1989.

———, and Burt Nanus. *Leaders, The Strategy for Taking Charge.* New York: Harper & Row, 1985.

Bierstadt, R. "An Analysis of Social Power." *American Sociological Review,* 15 (1950): 730-738.

Birnbaum, Robert. *How Colleges Work.* San Francisco: Jossey-Bass, 1988.

Blau, P. M., and W. R. Scott. *Formal Organizations.* San Francisco: Chandler, 1962.

Brewster, Kingman. "The Politics of the Academy." *School and Society,* 1967.

Burns, J. M. *Leadership.* New York: Simon and Schuster, 1978.

———. *The Power to Lead.* New York: Simon and Schuster, 1984.

Clark, B. R. "Organizational adaptation and precarious values: a case study." *American Sociology Review,* 21 (1956): 327–336.

Cohen, A. R. "The Effects of Situational Structure and Individual Self-Esteem on Threat-oriented Reactions to Power." Doctoral dissertation, University of Michigan, Ann Arbor, 1953.

Cohen, A. R. "Situational Structure, Self-Esteem, and Threat-Oriented Reactions to Power." *Studies in Social Power,* edited by D. Cartwright. Ann Arbor, MI: University of Michigan Institute for Social Research, 1959.

Collanos, P. A., and L. R. Anderson. "Effect of Perceived Expertness upon Creativity of Members of Brainstorming Groups." *Journal of Applied Psychology,* 2 (1969): 159-163.

Cowley, W. H. *Presidents, Professors, and Trustees.* San Francisco: Jossey-Bass, 1980.

Cox, A. J. *The Making of an Achiever.* New York: Dodd-Mead, 1985.

Davis, W. E. "Presidential Perspectives. That Revolving Door is Breaking Up That Old Gang of Mine—NASLGC, Presidential Tenures in the 80s." *The Green Sheet*, (1-4). Washington, DC: NASLCG, 1988.

Dornbusch, S. M., and W. R. Scott. *Evaluation and the Exercise of Authority: A Theory of Control Applied to Divers Organizations*. San Francisco: Jossey-Bass, 1975.

Dressel, Paul L. *Administrative Leadership*. San Francisco: Jossey-Bass, 1981.

Epstein, L. D. *Governing the University*. San Francisco: Jossey-Bass, 1984.

Falbo, T. "Multidimensional Scaling of Power Strategies." *Journal of Personality and Social Psychology*, 35 (1957): 537-547.

Fiedler, F. E. *A Theory of Leadership Effectiveness*. New York: McGraw-Hill, 1967.

————, G. E. O'Brien, and D. R. Ilgen. "The Effect of Leadership upon the Performance and Adjustment of Volunteer Teams Operating in Successful Foreign Environment." *Human Relations*, 22 (1969): 503-514.

Fisher, James. L. *The Power of the Presidency*. New York: Macmillan: 1984.

————, Martha Tack, and Karen Wheeler. *The Effective College President*. New York: ACE/Macmillan, 1988.

————, and Gary Quehl (ed.), *The President and Fundraising*. New York: ACE/Macmillan, 1989.

Foa, U. G., and E. B. Foa. *Societal Structures of the Mind*. Springfield, IL: C. C. Thomas, 1975.

French, J. R. P., W. Morrison, and G. Levinger. "Coercive Power and Forces Affecting Conformity." *Journal of Abnormal Social Psychology*, 61 (1960): 93-101.

————, and B. Raven. "The Bases of Social Power." *Studies of Social Power,* edited by D. Cartright. Ann Arbor, MI: University of Michigan, Institute for Social Research, 1959.

————, and R. Snyder. "Leadership and Interpersonal Power." *Studies in Social Power*, edited by D. Cartright. Ann Arbor, MI: University of Michigan, Institute for Social Research, 1959.

Galbraith, J. K. *The Anatomy of Power*. New York: Houghton-Mifflin, 1983.

Gardner, J. W. *The Nature of Leadership Series*. Independent Sector, Washington, DC, 1990.

Geertz, Clifford. *Local Knowledge*. New York: Basic Books, 1983.

Gilley, J. Wade, K. A. Fulmer, and S. J. Reithlingshoefer. *Searching for Academic Excellence*. New York: Macmillan, 1986.

Godfrey, E. P., F. E. Fiedler, and D. M. Hall. *Boards, Management and Company Success*. Danville, IL: Interstate, 1959.

Goodstadt, B., and L. A. Hjelle. "Power to the Powerless." *Journal of Personality and Social Psychology*, 27 (1973): 190-196.

————, and D. Kipnis. "Situational Differences in the Use of Power. *Journal of Applied Psychology*, 54 (1970): 201-207.

Green, Madeleine F. *Leaders for a New Era*. New York: Macmillan, 1988.

Greenleaf, R. K. *Servant Leadership*. New York: The Paulist Press, 1977.

Hall, J., and J. R. Hawker. *Power Management Inventory*. The Woodlands, Texas: Teleometrics International, 1981.

Hesburgh, T. M. "The College Presidency." *Change*, 11 (4): 43-47, 1979.

————. "Academic Leadership" *Leaders in Leadership*, edited by J. L. Fisher and M. W. Tack. San Francisco: Jossey-Bass, 1988.

Hill, W. "The validation and extension of Fiedler's theory of leadership effectiveness." *Academic Management Journal*, 12 (1969): 33-47.

Hollander, E. P. "Emergent Leadership and Social Influences" *Leadership and Interpersonal Behavior*, edited by L. Patrullo and B. M. Bass. New York: Holt, Rinehart, and Winston, 1961.

————. *Leadership Dynamics: A Practical Guide to Effective Relationships*. New York: Free Press, 1978.

House, R. J. "A 1976 Theory of Charismatic Leadership." in J. G. Hunt, and L. L. Larson. (ed.) *Leadership: The Cutting Edge*. Carbondale: Southern Illinois University Press, 1977.

Hunt, J. G. "Fiedler's Leadership Contingency Model: An Empirical Test in Three Organizations." *Organizational Behavior and Human Preference*, 2 (1967): 290-308.

Hurwitz, J. I., A. F. Zander, and B. Hymovitch. "Some Effects of Power on the Relations Among Group Members." In D. Cartwright and A. Zander (eds.), *Group Dynamics*. Evanston, IL: Row, Peterson, 1953.

Iverson, M. A. "Personality Impression of Punitive Stimulus Persons of Differential Status." *Journal of Abnormal and Social Psychology*, 68 (1964): 617-626.

Jones, E. E. *Integration*. New York: Appleton-Century-Crofts, 1964.

————, K. J. Gergen, P. Gumpert, and J. W. Thibaut. "Some Conditions Affecting the Use of Ingratiation to Influence Performance Evaluation." *Journal of Personality and Social Psychology*, 1 (1965): 613-625.

Jones, R. E., and E. E. Jones. "Optimum Conformity as an Ingratiation Tactic." *Journal of Personality and Social Psychology*, 32 (1964): 436–458.

Julian, J. W. "Leader and Group Behavior as Correlates of Adjustment and Performance in Negotiation Groups. *Dissertation Abstract*, 24 (1964): 646.

————, E. P. Hollander, and C. R. Regula. "Endorsement of the Group Spokesman as a Function of His Source of Authority, Competence and Success." *Journal of Personality and Social Psychology*, 11 (1969): 42-49.

Kanter, R. M. *The Change Masters*. New York: Simon & Schuster, 1983.

————. *Men and Women of the Corporate World*. New York: Basic Books, 1977.

Katz, D. "Patterns of Leadership." *Handbook of Political Psychology*, edited by J. N. Knutson. San Francisco: Jossey-Bass, 1973.

Kerr, Clark. *Presidents Make a Difference*. New York: Carnegie Corporation, 1984.

————, and Marian L. Gade, *The Many Lives of Academic Presidents*. Washington, DC: AGB, 1986.

Kipnis, D. *The Powerholders*. Chicago: The University of Chicago Press, 1976.

————, and R. Vanderveer. "Ingratiation and the Use of Power." *Journal of Personality and Social Psychology*, 26 (1971): 245-250.

————, and D. Wagner. "Character Structure and Response to Leadership." *Journal of Experimental Research in Personality*, 1 (1967): 16-24.

Kotter, J. P. "Power, Dependence, and Effective Management." *Harvard Business Review*, 55 (4): 125-136, 1977.

——. *The General Managers*. New York: Free Press, 1982.

——. *The Leadership Factor: What It Takes to Attract, Develop, Retain, and Motivate the Best Management Talent*. New York: Free Press, 1988.

——. *Power and Influence*. New York: Free Press, 1985.

Lawler, E. E. *Pay and Organizational Effectiveness*. New York: McGraw-Hill, 1971.

Machiavelli, N. *The Prince*. New York: Mentor Books, 1952.

McClelland, D. C. "The Two Faces of Power." *Journal of International Affairs*, 24 (1969): 141-154.

——, and D. H. Burnham, "Power is the Great Motivator." *Harvard Business Review*, 54 (1976): 100-110.

Milgram, S. "Some Conditions of Obedience and Disobedience to Authority." *Human Relations*, 18 (1965): 57-76.

Mills, T. M. "Power Relations in Three-Person Groups." *American Sociological Review* 18 (1953): 351-357.

Mortimor, K. P., and T. R. McConnell. *Sharing Authority Effectively*. San Francisco: Jossey-Bass, 1978.

Mott, P. E. "Power, Authority and Influence." *The Structure of Community Power*, edited by M. Aiken and P. E. Mott. New York: Random House, 1970.

Murdoch, P. "Development of Contractual Norms in a Dyad." *Journal of Personality and Social Psychology*, 6 (1967): 206-211.

Nason, John. *Presidential Assessment*. Washington, DC: Association of Governing Boards of Colleges and Universities, 1984.

Neustadt, R. E. *Presidential Power*. New York: John Wiley & Sons, 1960.

Parks, D. J. "Create a Vision, Build a Consensus, Be an Effective Leader." *The Clearing House*, 60 (1986): 88-90.

Patchen, M. "The Locus and Basis of Influence on Organizational Decisions." *Organization of Behavioral Human Performance*, 11 (1974): 195-221.

Pepitone, A. "Attributions of Causality, Social Attitudes, and Cognitive Matching Processes." In R. Taigiuri and L. Petrullo (eds.), *Person Perception and Interpersonal Behavior*. Stanford, CA: Stanford University Press, 1958.

Peters, T., and N. Austin. *A Passion for Excellence*. New York; Random House, 1985.

——, and R. H. Waterman, Jr. *In Search of Excellence*. New York: Random House, 1982.

Pettigrew, A. "Information Control as a Power Source." *Sociology*, 6 (1972): 187-204.

Pfeffer, J. *Power in Organizations*. New York: Ballinger, 1981.

Pruitt, G. A. *A Blueprint for Leadership: The American College Presidency*. (Doctoral dissertation) Union Graduate School (Ohio), 1974.

Raven, B. H. "The Comparative Analysis of Power and Influence." *Perspectives on Social Power*, edited by J. T. Tedeschi. Chicago: Aldine, 1974.

——, and A. W. Kruglanski. "Conflict and Power." *The Structure of Conflict*, edited by P. Swingle. New York: Academic Press, 1970.

Riesman, David, and Judith McLaughlin. "A Primer on the Use of Consultants in Presidential Recruitment." *Change*, 16 (6) 1984: 12–23.

Rubin, I. M., and M. Goldman. "An Open System Model of Leadership Performance." *Organizational Behavior and Human Performance*, 3 (1968): 143-156.

Schlesinger, A. M., Jr. *The Age of Roosevelt, Vol. 2: The Coming of the New Deal.* Boston: Houghton-Mifflin, 1959.

Schroder, H. M., S. Streufert, and D. C. Weeden. "The Effect of Structural Abstractness in Interpersonal Stimuli on the leadership role." Princeton, NJ: Princeton University, Office of Naval Research Technical Report No. 3, 1964.

Scott, E. L. *Leadership Perceptions of Organization.* Columbus, OH: Ohio State University Bureau of Business Research, 1956.

Seeman, M. *Social Status and Leadership—The Case of the School Executive.* Ohio State University. Educational Research Monograph No. 35, 1960.

Shaw, E. P. "The Social Distance Factor and Management." *Personnel Administration*, 28 (1956): 29-31.

Shirley, R. "Strategic Planning: An Overview." *Successful Strategic Planning*, edited by Douglas W. Steeples. San Francisco: Jossey-Bass, 1988.

Shepherd, C., and I. R. Weschler. "The Relationship between Three Interpersonal Variables and Communication Effectiveness: A Pilot Study." *Sociometry*, 18 (1955): 103-110.

Sherif, M., B. J. White, and O. J. Harvey. Status in Experimentally Produced Groups. *American Journal of Sociology*, 60 (1955): 370-379.

Slusher, E. A., G. L. Rose, and K. J. Roering. "Commitment of Future Interaction and Relative Power under Conditions of Interdependence." *Journal of Conflict Resolution*, 22 (1978): 282-298.

Smith, P. B. *Groups Within Organizations.* New York: Harper & Row, 1973.

Swingle, P. "Exploitative Behavior in Non-Zero-Sum Games." *Journal of Personality and Social Psychology*, 16 (1970): 121-132.

Tead, O. *The Art of Leadership.* New York: McGraw-Hill, 1935.

Tedeschi, J. T., S. Lindskold, J. Horai, and J. P. Gahagan. "Social Power and the Credibility of Promises." *Journal of Personality and Social Psychology*, 13 (1969): 253–261.

Thiagarajan, K. M., and S. D. Deep. "A Study of Supervisor-Subordinate Influence and Satisfaction in Four Cultures." *Journal of Social Psychology*, 82 (1970): 173-180.

Thibaut, J. W., and C. L. Gruder. "Formation of Contractual Agreements Between Parties of Unequal Power." *Journal of Personality and Social Psychology*, 11 (1969): 59-65.

Thwing, C. F. *The College President.* New York: Macmillan, 1926.

Torrance, E. P. "Some Consequences of Power Differences in Permanent and Temporary Groups." In P. Hare, E. F. Borgotta, and R. F. Bales (eds.), *Small Groups*, New York: Knopf, 1955.

Townsend, R. "Townsend's Third Degree in Leadership." *Across the Board*, 22 (6) 48-52, 1985.

Vaughn, G. B. *Leadership in Transition.* New York: ACE/Macmillan, 1989.

Walker, D. E. *The Effective Administrator*. San Francisco: Jossey-Bass, 1979.

Weber, M. *The Theory of Social and Economic Organization*. Translated by M. Henderson and T. Parsons. New York: Oxford University Press, 1947.

Wells, H. B. *Being Lucky: Reminiscences and Reflections*. Bloomington, IN: Indiana University Press, 1980.

Wenrich, J. W. "Can the President be All Things to All People?" *Community and Junior College Journal*, 51 (2) (1980): 36-40.

Whetten, D. A. "Effective Administrators: Good Management on College Campuses. *Change*, 16 (8) 1984: 38-43.

————, and K. S. Cameron. "Administrative Effectiveness in Higher Education." *Review of Higher Education*, 9 (1985): 35-49.

Zander, A., and T. Curtis. "Effects of Social Power on Aspiration Setting and Striving." *Journal of Abnormal Social Psychology*, 64 (1962): 63-74.

Index